A

Special Edition

of

# Walk as He Walked

and

# Coming Home

for

USA

# OM USA
# Short-term Missions

Transforming Lives and Communities

Our Purpose: OM's role in the Body of Christ is to motivate, develop, and equip people for world evangelization, and to strengthen and help plant churches, especially among the unreached in the Middle East, Europe, and South and Central Asia

## OPERATION MOBILIZATION

Toll Free: 800.899.0432
global.challenge.usa@om.org
www.usa.om.org

Short-term missions
285 Lynnwood Ave.
Tyrone, Georgia 30290

# Walk As He Walked

14 Devotions for a Successful Missions Trip

*He that saith he abideth in him ought himself*
*also so to walk, even as He walked.*
1 John 2:6

A Biblical Focus for Spiritual Growth

Developed and written by
Howard and Bonnie Lisech

Editorial Assistance
Jaye Hughes

additional copies may be ordered from
Deeper Roots Publications

E-Mail: DeeperRoots@aol.com

www.DeeperRoots.com

Publications available from Deeper Roots Publications at www.DeeperRoots.com

## SHORT-TERM RESOURCES

Pre–Field Preparation - 7 & 14 day Editions – Lisech
Walk as He Walked - 50 day Edition – Lisech
Walk as He Walked - 30 day Edition – Lisech
Walk as He Walked - 21 day Edition – Lisech
Walk as He Walked - 14 day Edition – Lisech
Abide in the Vine - 50 day Edition – Lisech
Abide in the Vine - 21 day Edition – Lisech
Abide in the Vine - 14 day Edition – Lisec
Ripe for Harvest - 21 day Edition – Lisech
Ripe for Harvest - 14 day Edition – Lisech
Coming Home book 1 (previously fishers of men) - 14 day Overseas Return Edition – Lisech
Coming Home Again book 2 - 14 day Returning From Overseas Edition – Lisech
Reentry Guide For Short Term Mission Leaders – Chinn
Before You Go - A Short Term Missions Manual – Erickson

## BIBLE CURRICULUM RESOURCES

Rooted & Grounded – 10-12th Grade & Adult Bible Curriculum – Lisech & Harris
Discovering Our Amazing God – 7-9th Grade Curriculum – Harris & Lisech
Discovering Who I Am In Christ 7-9th Grade Bible Curriculum – Harris & Lisech
Discovering Christlike Habits 7-9th Grade Bible Curriculum – Harris & Lisech
Firm Foundations – 4-5th Grade Children's Bible Curriculum – McLlwain/Everson (NTM)

Walked as He Walked -
14 Devotional Bible Studies - ISBN 1-930547-03-x     978-1-930547-03-2
12 Devotional Bible Studies - ISBN 1-930547-02-1,    978-1-930547-02-5
30 Devotional Bible Studies - ISBN 1-930547-01-3,    978-1-930547-01-8
50 Devotional Bible Studies - ISBN 1-930547-00-5,    978-1-930547-00-1

Since 1993, we have been writing and publishing short-term missions devotional Bible studies for those who are going to and returning from cross-cultural areas to minister to people who need the good news of Jesus Christ. *Pre-Field Preparation, Walk as He Walked, Abide in The Vine, Ripe for Harvest, Coming Home* (formerly *Fishers of Men),* and *Coming Home AGAIN* are collections of concepts, life principles, and personal insights that we have developed into short devotional studies taken from God's Word.

The Lord revealed some of the truths included in this series during several years of missionary training and overseas field assignment as missionaries in Papua New Guinea. We learned other life-changing lessons through personal Bible study, deep spiritual need, during ill health, and through redeployment to a stateside ministry.

While serving as leaders of a successful short-term mission program for many years, we focused on mobilizing and training North American Christians to have a vision for the world. We gained additional insights observing and teaching hundreds of short-term missionaries during pre-field training and reentry seminars. Other insights came as a result of discipling and teaching in our local church. These studies are a result of our personal search and desire to live and model the type of Christianity that works in every circumstance of life.

Personal leadership of six summer missions teams in Nepal, Belize, and Ecuador, combined with travel to Haiti, Bolivia, Mexico, and Guatemala reinforced the importance of making God's Word a priority. Originally targeted for short termers, we have seen these studies encourage and challenge those ministering overseas and many other Christians here at home! We praise God for His Word, wisdom, patience, and incredible faithfulness to us over the years. We desire that these materials will be a tremendous encouragement to others to walk with the Lord regardless of the challenges and circumstances of life.

*Pre-Field Preparation* can help anyone that desires to prepare their heart for significant ministry in another culture. *Walk as He Walked, Abide in The Vine,* and *Ripe for Harvest* are designed for use during the overseas portion of your trip. *Coming Home–Reentry Devotions for a Successful Return* and *Coming Home AGAIN* were born from our desire to help people come home successfully, readjust, and continue getting to know God as a person! They are highly recommended as ideal follow-up reentry studies. We have had many positive reports from both long and short-term workers as they reenter our home culture.

All credit and praise goes to our Lord!              *Howard & Bonnie Lisech*

# Elisabeth Elliot

Noted missionary speaker and author*
had this to say about

## Walk As He Walked
### (50 day edition)

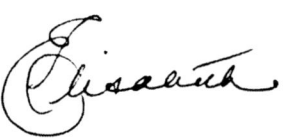

"The Liseches have had not only missionary experience,
but much experience of the faithfulness of God in deep
personal trials and afflictions.  They have blessed the lives of many young people
in training them to be faithful, humble, true followers of the One who loved us
and gave Himself for us.  I believe this little book would be deeply practical in the
preparation of anyone who honestly wants to follow the Crucified."

Warmly,

*Books by Elisabeth Elliot

"Through Gates of Splendor"
"Shadow of the Almighty"
"The Diary of Jim Elliot"
"The Savage my Kinsman"
"The Shaping of a Christian Family"
"The Liberty of Obedience"
"Discipline:  The Glad Surrender"
"Passion and Purity"
         and others

# Table of Contents

# KEEPING YOUR SPIRITUAL JOURNAL

Congratulations on your decision to travel, serve, and minister in another culture and location. What a tremendous opportunity to grow and mature. Keeping a journal will help you remember some of the things God does in you life.

As you complete the devotional studies, during your personal quiet time, make a conscious effort to listen to and be open to whatever God wants to teach you. Use the blank journal pages that follow each devotional to record your thoughts. Try to focus on and answer one or more of the following questions:

What is God teaching you about Himself, in terms of who He is? (His nature and character)

What is the Lord using to encourage you about His love and care for you?

What is God teaching you about His purpose and plan for you?

What is God teaching you about yourself?

What is God doing that may be causing you to reevaluate your life goals and values?

What person or concern is the Lord leading you to pray for?

What attitude changes or actions of obedience do you think God wants you to make?

Notes

Day 1

## HERE AT LAST!

**Gen. 12:1** *The LORD had said to Abram,*
*"Leave your country, your people and your father's household*
*and go to the land I will show you.* NIV

Perhaps you feel a little like Abraham right now. You are going to a "land that God will show you." Your country, home, and family are left behind. As a human being, Abraham must have had doubts on his long journey. Perhaps he thought, "Did God really tell me to go? Am I doing the right thing?" Many times Abraham must have remembered what God said and did for him to make his trip possible. Perhaps you feel this way right now. Write three things that God did specifically to prepare you for this experience:

1.


2.


3.


Use these things to remind and encourage yourself during the days ahead.

Gen. 12:2 "And I (God) will make of thee....." must have been Abraham's greatest encouragement. He decided not to miss God's life-changing promises. Gen. 12:4 "So he (Abraham) departed as the Lord had spoken unto him."

You are acting in obedience to God, and He will faithfully keep His promises to you.

What short phrase (or phrases) from these verses encourage you?

Ps. 56:3

Ps. 84:11

2 Tim. 1:7

What 3 things will you LACK, according to 2 Tim. 1:7, if you are fearful or timid?

1.

2.

3.

Read Ps. 27:1

In Hebrews 11:8, what were the major factors in Abraham's decision to go?

Discuss what we are instructed to do, according to 2 Cor. 10:5, when personal fears or careless talk interferes with our obedience to God.

What "knowledge of God" do we have to assure us that He will keep His promises? See Hebr. 10:23.

## PRAYER SUGGESTIONS

Confess any known sin. (Confession means that we agree with God about our sin.) Thank God for His forgiveness and complete cleansing (1 John 1:9). Share the special things you listed that encouraged you and thank God for each of them.

# INSIGHTS

Journaling your thoughts, perspectives, and experiences

Day 2

# WALK AS HE WALKED

**1 John 2:6** *He that saith he abideth in him ought himself also so to walk, even as he walked.* KJV

The Greek meaning for the word "abide" is "continue near or remain beside." We could paraphrase this verse: "If you say that you continue near or remain beside Christ, you should walk as He walked." The NIV translation for 1 John 2:6 reads: *Whoever claims to live in him must walk as Jesus did.* Christ is to be our example or role model. We see this teaching in 1 Pet. 2:21: ***For even hereunto were ye called: because Christ also suffered for us, leaving us an example, that ye should follow his steps:***

When we walk, we can take only one step at a time, one moment at a time. We are instructed to continue near or remain beside Christ step by step, moment by moment in our lives. See the verses below to understand the example that Christ left us.

1 John 1:5
What is true of God?

Light refers to God's perfection or holiness; God is without sin.
Darkness refers to sin—that which is ungodly.

1 John 1:6
By this verse, what is impossible if we walk in sin?

1 John 1:7

Who is this "one with another"?

In your own words, from the verses above, share what makes fellowship possible.

Are we able to walk as He walked, that is, without sinning? Read 1 John 1:8. 1 John 1:9 tells us what we need to do moment by moment in our lives as we recognize we are walking in sin. Read 1 John 1:9. What does God say happens to our sin when we confess? Why can we depend on this?

How much sin does God cleanse, on a moment-by-moment basis, as we confess or name the sin? (Confession means that we agree with God about our sin.) What does this mean to you?

If sin breaks our fellowship with God, then what restores it?

If there is no sin (because "all" of it has been cleansed due to confession), then are you walking as Christ walked in that moment?

Write and memorize 1 John 1:9.

## PRAYER SUGGESTIONS

Thank God for such a gracious and simple way to deal with our sin moment by moment. Ask God to help you be especially sensitive to His Holy Spirit, that you will be responsive when He reveals areas of sin in your life. Thank God for His <u>instant</u> forgiveness and total cleansing through 1 John 1:9. Praise God for instantly restoring your fellowship with Him.

# INSIGHTS

Journaling your thoughts, perspectives, and experiences

Day 3

# A PURE AND HOLY LIFE

**1Ths. 4:7**  *For God did not call us to be impure, but to live a holy life.*  NIV

Immorality has become an accepted way of life for many in our culture.  At every turn, we are bombarded by ungodly values seen on TV, in books, magazines, and disintegrating cultural values.  Believers must commit themselves to walk in purity and holiness, abstaining from all forms of sexual impurity, including lust and other perversions;
*For God did not call us to be impure, but to live a holy life.*  Read 1Ths. 4:1-8.

Reread verses 1-2.  Why did Paul give instructions on how to live?  On whose authority does he base his teaching?  [Note: to "please God" does not mean to obey in order to be accepted by Him or to gain His favor.  Your faith in Jesus Christ for salvation has already gained you God's acceptance and favor.  "Pleasing God" is living according to His will, which avoids consequences and brings spiritual blessings and growth.]  Who are you living to please right now?  God?  Yourself? Others?

Read Rom. 15:1 and 1 Ths. 2:4.  Whom does Paul say we should please, and not please?  Read John 8:29 to review Christ's example.  Whom did Christ please?

Read 1 Ths. 4:3-4, and write God's will for you, as found in these verses. [Note: the word "sanctify" means *separation to holiness in mind and body.* The word "abstain" means to *avoid or keep yourself from.* The word "fornication," in the KJV, means any *form of sexual impurity.*] Rewrite verse 3 in your own words.

Consider 2 Sam. 12:13-14 and 1 John 1:9. David had committed adultery and murder. What does Nathan say to David after he confessed and agreed with God about his sin? 1 John 1:9 shows us how we can have a "clean slate" with God on a moment by moment basis.

Remember, this does not always remove the consequences of our sin, but agreeing with God about our sin brings cleansing and restoration of our fellowship with Christ. Guilt never encourages us to be godly, but cleansing and forgiveness gives us a new beginning—a clean slate.

Read 1 Ths.4:5-6. [Note: the word "concupiscence" in the KJV means *lustful passions.*] What characterizes the life of the heathen? In your own words, write the holy behavior that is in contrast with the heathen life. Verse 5 says that the heathen do not know God personally. Why do you think maintaining a growing, deepening relationship with God would be vital to resisting sexual temptation for believers? Carefully review what you have written. Is this true in your life? What must you do to make this a reality in your life?

Read Ps. 119:9, Rom. 13:14, and Gal. 5:16. What practical insights did you get from each verse. How will you apply these in your life?

God does not only show concern for the Christian, but also for the other person involved in an immoral act. Reread 1 Ths. 4:7-8. What is the command and stern warning of this scripture? In verse 8, why do you think that Paul reminds us of the Holy Spirit? Read Eph 3:16 for help with your answer. If verse 16 is encouraging to you, write how.

## PRAYER SUGGESTIONS

Praise God for the privilege of knowing Him personally. Ask the Lord to continuously help you to grow deeper in your relationship with Him all of your life. Express to God your commitment to walk in the Spirit and maintain a pure and holy life that is well pleasing to Him. Praise the Lord that He is always ready to forgive your sins and give you a new beginning. Thank God for the Holy Spirit, who is the power of Christ in your life.

# INSIGHTS

Journaling your thoughts, perspectives, and experiences

Day 4

# LOVING OTHERS

### John 15:17 "These things I command you, that ye love one another." KJV

No doubt you know or will know a person who prompts emotions that are anything but loving. This person just doesn't arouse in us feelings of spontaneous approval and acceptance. In fact, we are really repulsed, and our first inclination is to have nothing to do with them. These are very honest feelings, and yet Christ says, **"These things I command you, that ye love one another."** (John 15:17) The problem is, how do we love when we don't feel like it?

Below are verses that assure us that God's command is to love. What do these verses have in common?

1 John 3:11

1 John 3:23

1 John 4:7

See Luke 6:27, 32, 35 to see how far love without feeling should go. What is the command of these verses? What does the last phrase of verse 35 mean to you?

How is this concept helpful to you in your relationships with others? From John 13:34-35, describe the importance of love for one another.

These are helpful verses, but they don't solve our problem—HOW can we love without the "feelings" of love? A phrase in 1 John 4:7 will help us: "for love is of God." Often we try to love with self-effort. God wants us to understand that He is the only One capable of loving the way we must love one another.

Write the phrase from John 15:5 that indicates that we are not capable of this love ourselves.

Read Gal. 5:22-23 and John 15:12. Where does this God-like love come from? Think carefully and write some ways that Christ loved us.

Read 1 John 3:16-18. Verse 16 tells us that we need to lay down our lives for others: dying to self, dying to our own wants, our desires, and even our plans moment by moment. This includes giving up the need for **feelings** in order to love.

According to verses 17-18, what does it take to love as God intended through Him?

Think of one person that you are presently struggling to love: a mom, dad, sister, brother, step-parent, friend, team member, or leader. Do one loving deed for them today. It might be writing a loving note or speaking a word of encouragement, having lunch with them so that you can get to know them better, or including this person in your activities. Write out your plan.

## Prayer Suggestions

Confess any known sin, including a lack of love. Praise God for Christ and His willingness to love through you. Thank Him for His willingness to die for you. Pray for God to love, through you, the person that He placed on your mind. Pray specifically for that person.

# INSIGHTS

Journaling your thoughts, perspectives, and experiences

Day 5

# BE A SERVANT

**Matt. 20:27** *And whosoever will be chief among you,*
*let him be your servant:* KJV

"And whoever wants to be first must be your slave—," says the NIV translation. Such an interesting principle; to be first you must be a servant to others. This concept is totally contrary to what we think is logical and what is taught by the world. Read Matt. 20:25-28 for the teaching of Jesus on this matter. Write the world's view on this subject.

Can you imagine what would happen if believers took this teaching as seriously as they should? Everyone would be serving each other with the same attitude that Jesus had. Record your thoughts.

Read Phil. 2:7. Write one area of life—an area of potential temptation to us—that Jesus gave up to become a servant. Share an area that you have given up, or need to give up, to be a servant.

One of the most beautiful examples of Christ's servanthood is found in John 13: 1-17. In the Jewish culture, washing the feet of his master's guests was the task of the lowliest servant. Walking on dirt roads wearing sandals made very dusty, dirty feet!

Read John 13:1-17.
You might have noticed that Jesus washed their feet *after* the meal. The washing of feet usually took place as the guests arrived. Not one of the disciples was willing to take on this lowly task—not even to wash the feet of Jesus.

Are you willing to serve others, even if it is not your appointed job?

According to verse 17, what is the result of a servant attitude and action?

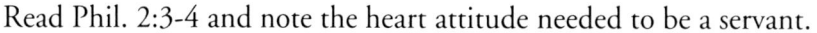

Read Phil. 2:3-4 and note the heart attitude needed to be a servant.

Note what changes need to take place in your life. What plan of action will you take to serve others?

## PRAYER SUGGESTIONS

Praise God for His unconditional love for you. Agree with God about any sin He has revealed to you through this lesson. Thank Him for His complete cleansing and the wonderful fellowship with Christ that has been restored. Share with God your need for dependence on Him as you seek to have the attitude of Christ—that of a humble servant.

# INSIGHTS

Journaling your thoughts, perspectives, and experiences

Day 6

# EXPECTATIONS

**Ps. 57:2** *I will cry unto God most high; unto God
that performeth all things for me.* KJV

Life's experiences don't always turn out the way we picture or think they will. In fact, at times it seems they never do! Our expectations are generally unrealistic, and these unrealistic expectations can lead us into disappointment, discouragement, and even anger. Our godly attitude can instantly change to one of ungodliness if our expectations are not met.

The Israelites had a wrong expectation. They anticipated that the long-awaited Messiah would be a conquering King and would remove the Romans by setting up His Kingdom on earth. The unexpected reality was a lowly servant that arrived in a manger. Their unmet expectation led them to reject the King of Kings.

What do you expect today? What if the situation is not as you anticipate? Perhaps your attitude will make you miss something special God has for you.

David writes about his attitude toward circumstances in Ps. 57:1-2. At the time he wrote these verses, he was fleeing for his life. King Saul sought to kill him.

What is David's attitude toward his circumstances?

What action does he take?

Where does David think these life situations are coming from?

What is God's reason for allowing these unexpected experiences? Hopefully, your circumstances are not as grave as David's. But many times the little things affect our attitudes the most. The same principles taught by David's life apply to us. See the following scriptures for further encouragement.

2 Sam. 22:31

In the King James Version of the Bible you will find the word "buckler." This word means "a shield or protection."

Rom. 8:28

Isa. 26:3

Prov. 16:3

Memorize the verse from the lesson that is most meaningful to you and recite it to someone on your team. Record the reference here.

When faced with unexpected life experiences, what steps will you now take to deal with your attitudes?

## PRAYER SUGGESTIONS

Share your negative attitudes, your disappointment, discouragement, and anger with your Lord. Confess that these are sin in your life, and thank God for His complete cleansing. Praise Him and thank Him that He is God and can be trusted in the big and little calamities of life.

## INSIGHTS
Journaling your thoughts, perspectives, and experiences

Day 7

# OBEY YOUR LEADERS

**Hebr. 13:17** *Obey your leaders and submit to their authority.*
*They keep watch over you as men who must give an account.*
*Obey them so that their work will be a joy, not a burden,*
*for that would be of no advantage to you.* NIV

The word *submit* means to "arrange under" and was originally a military term referring to the relations of a soldier to his commanding officer. The believer must consider another dimension with this obvious obedience—that of heart attitude. Submission cannot be forced; it must come freely by an act of choice determined by a decision to obey God from the heart.

Read Col. 3:17, 23 to discover the heart attitude from which submission must spring. What do these two verses require for submission to authority?

The key to this obedience is found in the direction of our submission. See the last two phrases of verse 23. When we obey and submit to our leaders with the right heart attitude, who are we really obeying?

Jesus is the greatest example of submission to authority. Read the verses listed and note the extent of Jesus' obedience to God the Father.

Matt. 26:39

John 5:30

Phil. 2:8

Who are your leaders?

Has your attitude toward these persons been an example of Christ?

If you said no, what steps will you take to change this attitude?

Read the following verses and write each command.

Titus 3:1-2

Eph. 6:5-6

Titus 2:9

Read each command again. Which of these are your strong points? Choose the ones you need to work on. Share your plan for improving in these areas.

## PRAYER SUGGESTIONS

Confess to your loving Lord any sin of disobedience to authority. Praise God for His protection and care for you. Thank Him for the example of Jesus' life. Ask God to help you to be a humble servant and to deal with the areas of need in your life. Thank Him for allowing you to obey Him by obeying the leaders that He places over you.

# INSIGHTS
Journaling your thoughts, perspectives, and experiences

Day 8

## "FORGIVE AS THE LORD FORGAVE YOU"

**Col. 3:13** *Bear with each other and forgive whatever grievances
you may have against one another.
Forgive as the Lord forgave you.* NIV

The Apostle Peter asked Jesus, "Lord, how many times shall I forgive my brother when he sins against me? Up to seven times?" Peter must have felt very noble suggesting seven times; it was commonly taught by the Jewish leaders that three times was enough to forgive. Jesus answers with a very large number that is symbolic for "unlimited forgiveness" by believers. We never have the right to refuse to forgive. Believers are commanded to forgive as many times as they are sinned against. Jesus teaches **why** we are to forgive others in Matt 18:21-35.

Read Matt. 18:21-27 (Note: Ten thousand talents is about ten million dollars.)
In these verses the King is a picture of God and the servant represents God's people who are sinners in need of forgiveness. Write in your own words the King's first action when he is faced with this debtor.

What behavior of the indebted servant causes the King to be merciful?

The King knows that the debt is too immense for the debtor to ever repay. What is the second action of the King?

Think about this total, unconditional forgiveness and freedom given by the King. Write your thoughts.

Compare Matthew 18:27 and Romans 6:23. Write about the immense debt that was yours and its cancellation by Christ's death and resurrection.

Jesus' teaching on forgiveness continues in Matthew 18:28-35. Read this portion. (Note: a hundred denarii was about fourteen dollars.) In verse 28 you will discover that the servant "left" the fellowship of the King. Compare the King's mercy and forgiveness with the servant's actions toward his fellow servant. What do you think Jesus is trying to say in His teaching about the unforgiving servant?

Read verse 34-35. If the torture for the unforgiving believer is "guilt," how do you think this affects him? What other sins come from not forgiving others who sin against you?

About verses 34-35: It is important for you to notice that this teaching was before the death of Christ. The cross of Christ canceled our debt forever and our sins were forgiven and forgotten by God. As it says in Hebrews 8:12, "*For I will forgive their wickedness and will remember their sins no more.*" When we are unforgiving, we are out of fellowship with Christ and we need to be obedient to confess our sin according to 1 John 1:9. Trusting in the power of the Holy Spirit we must forgive and love the person that sinned against us. Read 1 John 3:23 and Eph.4:32.

How must you forgive others? Is an unforgiving heart against a specific individual blocking your fellowship with Christ?

By faith, choose to forgive and love that person. What loving action will you take to express your forgiveness?

## PRAYER SUGGESTIONS

Praise the Lord for His mercy and grace in forgiving your immense debt of sin. Thank Him for expressing in actions His love by dying for you on the cross. Thank God that He forgave you and pardoned you unconditionally, canceling all your sin debt. Express to Him your thoughts about forgiving others.

# INSIGHTS

Journaling your thoughts, perspectives, and experiences

Day 9

# BE ANXIOUS FOR NOTHING

**Phil. 4:6** *Be careful for nothing;*
*but in every thing by prayer and supplication with thanksgiving*
*let your requests be made known unto God.* KJV

"Don't worry or be anxious about anything" is the wording we would use today. In this verse we find a command followed by the solution. In the world today the temptation to worry is indeed strong. Worry is said to be a leading cause of physical, emotional, and spiritual problems.

List the 3 greatest worries that you have at this time. Be honest.

1.

2.

3.

Write in your own words the command and the solution found in Phil. 4:6.

Read Prov. 3:5-8 and record what encourages you.

Read the following scriptures and write the command and the promise in your own words.

Ps. 55:22

Ps. 62:8

Ps. 73:21-26, 28

Ps. 115:9

1 Pet. 5:7

Phil.4:6 highlights the result of our obedience to God's commands. Review the commands, the solutions, and the promises you have written. Now write the results given in Phil 4:7.

## PRAYER SUGGESTIONS

As you begin your prayer to the Lord, try to identify and name your worries. After doing that, confess each of them to the Lord as sin. Thank Him for His cleansing, commands, and promises. Praise Him for the peace only He can give.

# INSIGHTS

Journaling your thoughts, perspectives, and experiences

Day 10
# TRIALS, PERSEVERANCE, GROWTH, AND JOY!

*James 1:2-4 Consider it pure joy, my brothers,
whenever you face trials of many kinds,
because you know that the testing of your faith develops perseverance.
Perseverance must finish its work so that you may be mature and complete,
not lacking anything.* **NIV**

Christians should desire growth. Trials and testing are a vital ingredient in the growth process. The will of God is that believers develop and mature. Perseverance is a tool God uses in this "growth" process. "Persevere" means to be patient, to persist or to continue unswervingly. We are not to regard trials and testing as negative; rather, they are to be viewed as positive life experiences that are directed by God for a deeper, more meaningful walk with Christ. This is the reason we can choose to have an attitude of joy in times of trial, because we know that spiritual growth is taking place in our lives.

Share how you feel about trials and testing in your life.

What is your approach to enduring trials?

If *perseverance* is the tool that God uses, what do you think happens to spiritual growth and maturing in our lives if we do <u>not</u> persevere with a joyful attitude during our trials? Note: it is not the trials that bring growth, but our reaction or perseverance during trials.

Read 1 Peter 1:3-9 and write the purpose of trials and testing.

What is revealed here about your faith?

What is the result of the refining process? Reread verse 8. What is our major reason for continuing in the faith?

Read Rom. 5:1-5. List that which is produced by perseverance. This "perseverance" or "patience" is produced in our lives by the Holy Spirit. The Holy Spirit produces the fruit of the Spirit (Gal. 5:21-23) through our lives as we walk in obedience to God moment by moment.

King David's approach to trials and suffering is found in Ps. 119:49-50. What did he do to have hope? What do you do to encourage yourself to persevere when you are involved in trials?

1 Peter 5:10 expresses the end results of trials, testing and the suffering that comes from them. Take time to think deeply about this verse. Share what encourages you about God Himself in this verse. Record the end result. Share your thoughts, any changes you need to make, and your plan to achieve these changes.

## PRAYER SUGGESTIONS

Share with God your desire to grow in your love for Him and mature in your faith. Express your reluctance toward or acceptance of trials and testings and your need to trust in His Word for comfort. Praise Him for the promises and encouragement found in His Word. Thank Him that the Holy Spirit will produce the fruit "joy" as you walk in obedience moment by moment.

# INSIGHTS

Journaling your thoughts, perspectives, and experiences

Day 11
# COMPLAINING—GOD TAKES IT PERSONALLY

**Phil. 2:14-15** *Do everything without complaining or arguing,*
*so that you may become blameless and pure,*
*children of God without fault in a crooked and depraved generation,*
*in which you shine like stars in the universe.* NIV

This verse is a very powerful command, but with an equally powerful promise. Read Philippians 2:14-15 three times and think carefully about every phrase. Write your thoughts about each phrase. Why do you think you would become "like stars that shine" if you obey the command of verse fourteen? What difference could this make in your life and the world watching you?

Philippians 2:13 gives us the reason we can have complete confidence that God is in control and that we have no valid reason ever to complain or argue. Write the reasons.

Scripture proves that <u>God takes complaining personally.</u> Read the following verses to see God's reaction to complaining by the children of Israel after God's great deliverance from Egypt. Their complaints are directed toward Moses, their leader, <u>but God took it personally.</u>

Num. 11:1-15

Num. 11:10-11

Num. 11:15

Write what you have observed in these scriptures about complaining. What effect does complaining have on leadership?  Share your thoughts.

Read the following verses for more insight.  You may want to read the context surrounding these verses.  Write what you learn about the Lord in these verses.

Num. 14:27

Num. 16:11

Read Proverbs 6:16, 19b.  In the NIV translation the word "dissension" is used, and in the KJV the word "discord" is used.  Both words mean "disagreement that brings about arguing."  It is very unusual that we grumble and complain in private.  Eventually the unconfessed sin of complaining is shared with someone, which leads to gossip and discord within a family,  group, or team of people.  The  Israelites were united in their complaints and God was not pleased.  Their grumbling was evidence of an ungodly attitude.  Sometimes in a group of people, grumbling is often started by just one person.

The following verses give us directions for the proper handling of a complaint.

Ps. 142:2


Eph. 5:20-21


1Ths. 5:16-18


Phil. 4:4-6


What impressed you during this study? Do you need to make some changes in your life in regards to complaining, arguing and grumbling? What steps will you take to bring about this change?


## PRAYER SUGGESTIONS

Confess any personal sin that currently hinders you from fellowship with Christ. Praise Him for His faithfulness as He forgives you and cleanses you from all unrighteousness. Share with God what you have learned in this study regarding needed changes that you desire for the Lord to make in your life. Express your trust in God who works in you to will and to act according to His good purpose.

# INSIGHTS

Journaling your thoughts, perspectives, and experiences

Day 12

# ALL FOR THE GLORY OF GOD

**Eph. 1:12** *That we should be to the praise of his glory, who first trusted in Christ.*
**NIV**

What is your purpose in life? Ephesians 1:12 tells us that a believer's purpose is to glorify God. Is this your life goal? Reread the verse above and note that it says we are to **BE** *to the praise of his glory*—not **DO** *to the praise of his glory.*

The following verses are an interesting study of men who were outwardly religious. They tried to "do" something to glorify God, but neglected their inner life.    Read Matt. 23:2,14-15, 23, 26-27. (Some translations omit verse 14.) List all the "right" things they did.

Even Jesus said they were outwardly clean.  It wasn't their performance that was necessarily wrong; it was their hearts.  Reread Matt. 23:27 for Jesus' opinion.  Now review verse 26.  What does Jesus tell them that they need to do?

These Pharisees were unsaved men.  What about believers?  Aren't we also prone to performance while neglecting the the inner life? Is "doing" wrong? No! But service must

flow from the heart of the believer who is cleansed and empowered by the Holy Spirit. Read the following verses and write what encourages you.
Ps. 51:6,7,12

Eph. 3:16

1 Cor. 10:31

Hosea 8:14a in the KJV says, *"For Israel hath forgotten his Maker, and buildeth temples."* Has "serving," "busyness," and "good works" taken the place of seeking to know God and to develop a close and meaningful relationship? Write your thoughts.

Underline the most neglected area or areas that you need to give attention to for the purpose of *"being* to the praise of His glory." Develop a plan that will help correct your present course. Carefully consider how to incorporate all of the following:

1. Take time to study and be with God in His Word to develop my spiritual life.

2. Confess my sinful attitudes on a moment-by moment basis, even when my works look outwardly spiritual.

3   Pray for my own growth with an open and teachable heart before God.

4.  Make good use of my time and avoid procrastination.

5.  Pray and seek the Lord's direction in decisions concerning what I choose to do in serving Him.

6.  Faithfully attend to growth opportunities toward which God has directed me. (Church, Sunday school, discipleship, Bible studies, accountability groups, etc.) (Add your own if you desire.)

**My plan:**

## Prayer Suggestions

Praise the Lord for making possible a deep and meaningful relationship with Him through His Word. Ask God to reveal to you any performance-oriented activity in which you are presently involved that hinders you from the deep, meaningful spiritual development that would glorify Him. Share with Him the need or needs you underlined. Ask him to help you carry out your plan to correct these needs.

# INSIGHTS

Journaling your thoughts, perspectives, and experiences

Day 13

# GOD IS FAITHFUL

**2Tim. 2:13** *if we are faithless, he will remain faithful,*
*for he cannot disown himself.* NIV

Faithfulness is a character trait of God. Believers are often unfaithful and untrustworthy. This is never true of God—He is always faithful. The above verse is of great comfort to believers. When we are not trusting in the Lord, which is the meaning of faithless, God remains faithful to His Word. In the King James Version the last phrase of the above verse is "He cannot deny himself." Yes, He is faithful and He *cannot* be any other way!

Take a few minutes and give some deep thought to 2 Tim. 2:13. Share your thoughts and observations.

Read the following verses. Write in your own words what you learn about God.

Lam. 3:22-23

Ps. 33:4

Deut. 7:9

Deut. 32:4

Num. 23:19

Titus 1:2

Hebr. 10:23

Hebr. 11:11

1 Pet. 4:19

1 John 1:9

Rev. 1:5

Think of a favorite promise that God gave you from His Word and what it means to you that God is faithful, even though you are sometimes lacking in faith. Share the promise and your thoughts.

What has encouraged you during this study? Has your thinking changed? If so, how?

## PRAYER SUGGESTIONS

Because God is faithful to forgive your sin, share with God by naming each personal sin that needs to be cleansed. Thank Him for His faithfulness to forgive you and purify you from *all* sin, moment by moment. Praise Him for His great and perfect love for you. Thank Him for being faithful even when you are not faithful. Praise Him by sharing what you wrote about Him in the questions above.

# INSIGHTS

Journaling your thoughts, perspectives, and experiences

Day 14

# THE REAL TREASURE

*Matt. 6:33* *But seek first his kingdom and his righteousness,*
*and all these things will be given to you as well.* NIV

One of the privileges of traveling overseas is meeting national believers who have very little in material wealth but stand out as people of great faith and joy. These believers usually share what they have graciously and sacrificially with others.

Our culture promotes accquiring wealth and material possessions as a high goal. This is "success" we are told, and even believers are tempted to believe it. Yet we see little joy in the life of most believers as a result. We need to take very seriously the teaching of Matthew 6:19-34.

Read Matt. 6:19-21. According to verse 19, what is true of earthly treasures? Have you ever lost a treasure in this way?

According to verse 21, how does your focus for life affect your heart? Write some consequences you can think of that come from allowing material wealth to be the primary goal of your life.

Read Matt. 6:22-23 and see how Jesus answers your last question. On what have you focused your eye in this life? Jesus is saying that either our spiritual sight is healthy and spiritual when focused on heavenly treasure, or it is deceived and distorted when our goal is earthly treasure. Write your thoughts.

Read Matt. 6:24. What problem arises when you pursue the goal of attaining wealth at the same time as you pursue the goal of obeying and serving God?

Read Matt. 6:25-32. What comfort does Jesus give us in these verses? According to verse 32, who are believers like when they worry about material possessions? What place does worry have in a believer's life? How does "discontentment" enter into this for the believer?

Read Matt. 6:33-34 and write out the command and promise Jesus gave. In your opinion, what is the greatest problem believers face in trying to obey this command and accept the promise? What sins are taken care of when we are obedient?

Just what is this "real" treasure? Read the following verses and note what God considers to be "real" wealth.

1 Tim. 6:17-19

2 Cor. 4:6-7

Col. 2:2-3

Has this study changed your life goal? If so, in what way? What changes are you planning to make? Write your thoughts.

## PRAYER SUGGESTIONS

Praise God for treasures that are eternal and fulfilling. Share with Him any personal unconfessed sin that has hindered your pursuit of "real" wealth. Thank the Lord for supplying good things for you to enjoy. Ask His help in seeking and discovering treasure that is hidden in wisdom, knowledge, and understanding of Christ through the work of the Holy Spirit in your life.

# INSIGHTS

Journaling your thoughts, perspectives, and experiences

# INSIGHTS

Journaling your thoughts, perspectives, and experiences

# INSIGHTS
Journaling your thoughts, perspectives, and experiences

# INSIGHTS
Journaling your thoughts, perspectives, and experiences

# Coming Home

## Reentry Devotions For Successful Return
### Book 1


Belongs To

_____

**A Deeper Roots Publication**

# Coming Home

## Reentry Devotions for a Successful Return

### 14 Devotional Bible Studies
### with reentry and debrief questions

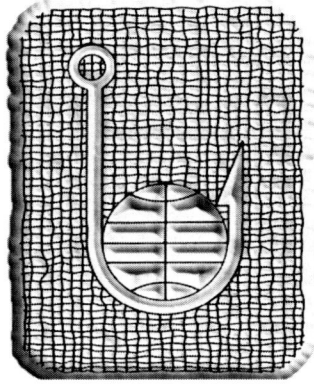

Developed and Written by
Howard and Bonnie Lisech

additional copies may be ordered from (see order blank)
Deeper Roots Publications
2100 Red Gate Rd
Orlando, FL 32818
(407) 293-8666
or
E-Mail: DeeperRoots@aol.com

www.deeperroots.com

Publications available from Deeper Roots Publications at www.DeeperRoots.com

## SHORT-TERM RESOURCES
PRE–FIELD PREPARATION  -  7 & 14 DAY EDITIONS  –  LISECH
WALK AS HE WALKED  -  50 DAY EDITION  –  LISECH
WALK AS HE WALKED  -  30 DAY EDITION  –  LISECH
WALK AS HE WALKED  -  21 DAY EDITION  –  LISECH
WALK AS HE WALKED  -  14 DAY EDITION  –  LISECH
ABIDE IN THE VINE  -  50 DAY EDITION  –  LISECH
ABIDE IN THE VINE  -  30 DAY EDITION  –  LISECH
ABIDE IN THE VINE  -  21 DAY EDITION  –  LISECH
ABIDE IN THE VINE  -  14 DAY EDITION  –  LISEC
RIPE FOR HARVEST  -  21 DAY EDITION  –  LISECH
RIPE FOR HARVEST  -  14 DAY EDITION  –  LISECH
COMING HOME BOOK 1  (PREVIOUSLY FISHERS OF MEN)  -  14 DAY OVERSEAS RETURN EDITION  –  LISECH
COMING HOME AGAIN  BOOK 2  -  14 DAY RETURNING FROM OVERSEAS EDITION  –  LISECH
REENTRY GUIDE FOR SHORT TERM MISSION LEADERS  –  CHINN
BEFORE YOU GO  -  A SHORT TERM MISSIONS MANUAL  –  ERICKSON

## BIBLE CURRICULUM RESOURCES
ROOTED & GROUNDED  –  10-12TH GRADE & ADULT BIBLE CURRICULUM  –  LISECH & HARRIS
DISCOVERING OUR AMAZING GOD  –  7-9TH GRADE CURRICULUM  –  HARRIS & LISECH
DISCOVERING WHO I AM IN CHRIST  7-9TH GRADE BIBLE CURRICULUM  –  HARRIS & LISECH
DISCOVERING CHRISTLIKE HABITS  7-9TH GRADE BIBLE CURRICULUM  –  HARRIS & LISECH
DISCOVERING CHRISTLIKE CHARACTER  7-9TH GRADE BIBLE CURRICULUM  –  HARRIS & LISECH

FIRM FOUNDATIONS  –  3-4TH GRADE  CHILDREN'S BIBLE CURRICULUM  –  MCLLWAIN/EVERSON (NTM)

Scripture quotations designated (KJV) are from the King James Version

Scripture quotations designated (NIV) are from the The Holy Bible,
New International Version, ©1978 by the New York International Bible Society, published by the Zondervan Corporation

COMING HOME  -  14 Devotional Bible Studies for Reentry

# Table of Contents

To:

Those who have, by faith, crossed into other cultures to serve
and present the claims of Christ to those who have not yet
heard the truth.

## To Our Special Thanks To

Lisa Espineli Chinn
for encouragement, assistance, and insight

Rick Madsen
for editorial perspective and detail

Since 1993, we have been writing and publishing short-term missions devotional Bible studies for those who are going to and returning from cross-cultural areas to minister to people who need the good news of Jesus Christ. *Pre-Field Preparation, Walk as He Walked, Abide in The Vine, Ripe for Harvest, Coming Home* (formerly *Fishers of Men*), and *Coming Home AGAIN* are collections of concepts, life principles, and personal insights that we have developed into short devotional studies taken from God's Word.

The Lord revealed some of the truths included in this series during several years of missionary training and overseas field assignment as missionaries in Papua New Guinea. We learned other life-changing lessons through personal Bible study, deep spiritual need, during ill health, and through redeployment to a stateside ministry.

While serving as leaders of a successful short-term mission program for many years, we focused on mobilizing and training North American Christians to have a vision for the world. We gained additional insights observing and teaching hundreds of short-term missionaries during pre-field training and reentry seminars. Other insights came as a result of discipling and teaching in our local church. These studies are a result of our personal search and desire to live and model the type of Christianity that works in every circumstance of life.

Personal leadership of six summer missions teams in Nepal, Belize, and Ecuador, combined with travel to Haiti, Bolivia, Mexico, and Guatemala reinforced the importance of making God's Word a priority. Originally targeted for short termers, we have seen these studies encourage and challenge those ministering overseas and many other Christians here at home! We praise God for His Word, wisdom, patience, and incredible faithfulness to us over the years. We desire that these materials will be a tremendous encouragement to others to walk with the Lord regardless of the challenges and circumstances of life.

*Pre-Field Preparation* can help anyone that desires to prepare their heart for significant ministry in another culture. *Walk as He Walked, Abide in The Vine,* and *Ripe for Harvest* are designed for use during the overseas portion of your trip. *Coming Home–Reentry Devotions for a Successful Return* and *Coming Home AGAIN* were born from our desire to help people come home successfully, readjust, and continue getting to know God as a person! They are highly recommended as ideal follow-up reentry studies. We have had many positive reports from both long and short-term workers as they reenter our home culture.

All credit and praise goes to our Lord!                    *Howard & Bonnie Lisech*

# LISA ESPINELI CHINN
### Cross-Cultural Trainer and Consultant

# COMING HOME
## &
# COMING HOME AGAIN

"Who is there for the returning missionary on their first, second, or third reentry?

Family, friends, and the church become key support people who will listen, understand, and encourage the eager and tired returnee. After the initial sharing and euphoria are over, who stays on to care and listen?

The Liseches have skillfully and sensitively woven together the principles of God's Word and the issues of readjustment and reentry into each of these reentry studies.

*Coming Home–Reentry Devotions for a Successful Return* Book 1
takes the readers to the One who is constantly there to comfort and guide. It is a refreshing addition to the meager reentry resources in missions today. This is a 'must' Bible study guide for everyone returning home after a time of service in another setting or country.

*Coming Home Again–Reentry Devotions for Another Successful Return* Book 2
is recommended if you have already completed **Coming Home** (previously titled *Fishers of Men*). **Coming Home Again** will be so very helpful as you process another overseas experience."

> Lisa Espineli Chinn is a cross-cultural trainer with many years of training short term and career missionaries. She is currently serving with InterVarsity Christian Fellowship/USA as the National Director of International Student Ministries.

Author,
"*REENTRY GUIDE FOR SHORT-TERM MISSION LEADERS*": a reentry resource for STM leaders
"*THINK HOME*": a reentry guide for returning Christian International students
"*CUSTOMS AND CULTURE*": A very helpful simulation game for those who are reentering their culture

# Coming Home

As you return from serving in another culture, you are involved in what is called the "reentry process." People returning from overseas service don't usually expect to have to "reenter" their own culture. Remember this: you have experienced significantly different people and places and you have changed. This experience will continue to change your attitude, outlook, and life values. You will have new perspectives and a new appreciation for what God is doing in the world

and how you "fit." Some of the cross-cultural relationships that you formed will influence you forever. It may take months or even years for you to understand the total impact. The magnitude and effect of your cross-cultural experience may elude you for a time, and you may even deny that you are different. Then, after a period of time, you will begin to realize and appreciate the changes in your perspective of the Lord, and of the peoples of the World that He loves.

Our Lord wants to conform us to the image of Christ. As you return to your home, work, neighborhood, church, or your school, you will have unique opportunities to share your overseas experience. Share with enthusiasm, love, and compassion. However, if you encounter apathy or insensitivity, *don't allow yourself to be critical*. Show how God is changing you from who you were, to the person He wants you to be—*a fisher of men*—a World Christian. Share how you are beginning to see the peoples of the world more from God's perspective than from your own. Choose to serve rather than being served. Talk is cheap, but your actions will prove your new love and vision.

Your overseas trip is over. It was only a first step. Remember how frightening it was to take that step of faith? Consider the impact in your life. You wouldn't have missed it. The second step of your journey begins as you choose to obey, grow, and get to know God as a friend, a loving Father, and most importantly as LORD. To grow significantly, you will need to exercise discipline. It will take some effort on your part. The choice is up to you. Don't allow yourself to fall into old patterns and routines. As you grow and mature, you will be able to understand God's will for you much more clearly. The Word of God is the key to unlocking God's plan for your life. Don't misplace your key - *choose* to read and meditate on scripture as you continue to spend quality time in His Word.

# A Reentry Letter

When Peter, Edmund, Lucy, and Susan stepped out of the wardrobe\*, they were shocked to find out that no one seemed to know anything about the world from which they had just returned. In Narnia, they had experienced the breathtaking beauty of the place and its citizens; they had discovered things about themselves they had not known before; they had conquered evil; they had known love on new and different levels; they had met friends that had challenged all of their normal ways of thinking. They had been important people there. They had completely become a part of that world. So when they walked out of the wardrobe, they were shocked to find their changes were unapparent to everyone around them. When to the children, the changes they saw in themselves were so great that they were now almost completely different people.

We recently had the privilege of having 4 American college guys come live, work, and serve with us. Our boys (as we lovingly called them) faced every challenge head-on without complaint. They dove into the culture and lifestyle of our area 100%. They made friends with many Chinese students, became a part of the host homes that they lived in, and made every effort to encourage and help out the long-term team. Many people heard of Jesus and His sacrifice this summer because of their faithfulness in being both patient and bold. At the end of their time with us, during their debriefing time, we shared how returning to America can feel uncannily like the Peter, Edmund, Lucy, and Susan must have felt when they stepped out of the wardrobe. As we prepared the guys to return to America, we realized that we were also talking to ourselves. Within weeks of our short-term guys leaving, nearly our entire team returned to their home countries for our home-leave (furlough, home assignment) times.

And I must say, we were right! It feels exactly like I've stepped out of my "wardrobe life" into another one. I often ponder what a strange life I live as a missionary, and maybe one of the strangest parts is this thing called Home Leave. I've asked many questions in the month I've been back in America. Who am I? What am I supposed to do today? Why do I feel so awkward in situations that look so familiar?

\* *Narnia* - Disney Pictures, & *The Lion, the Witch, and The Wardrobe*, CS Lewis

# Coming Home

*But the hardest part for me has been transitioning community going from my place in the community of Chinese friends and team that I have worked so hard to foster back to my circle of family and friends here in America who I am used to missing from a distance. This has been a super hard transition to navigate, but the Lord has been faithful in granting strength. Also, my family and friends here have helped so much in being persistent and patient with me. I am thankful.*

*It has been so good for me to have chances to share about China and what the Lord is doing there. Living there, I have become so accustomed to the world around me that I've become a little blind to things that are good to remember. China is an AMAZING place. My Chinese friends are incredibly kind, patient, generous, and hospitable. I have learned so much from living there. I am thankful*

*Angie S.*

As Angie's letter illustrates, returning home is an uncertain time whether we have been gone for 2 weeks or 2 years. Often things just don't "feel" right and we ususally don't expect that.

　1. Things may have changed a little or a lot in your absence as you were immersed in another culture. Hundreds of little things change every day, but if we aren't here to adjust to them, they can make us feel out of touch.

　2. More importantly, YOU have changed. No matter how long or how short your immersion in another culture, you will be significantly different as you return home. Before you leave home, you can't realize how much the cross-cultural experience will impact you.

Several years ago I saw an illustration* depicting people going from their home culture as stick figures with SQUARES representing the values, ideals, and dreams of the home culture. The host culture was depicted by stick figures that were ROUND. Their roundness was the sum total of their values, ideals and dreams.

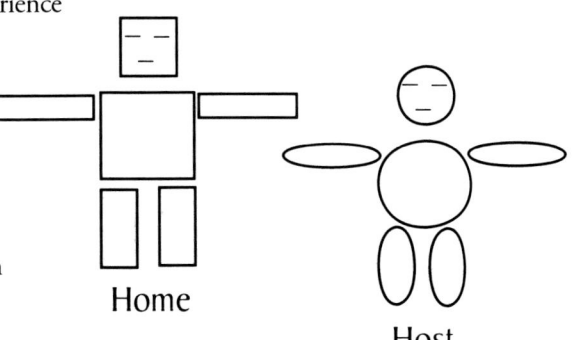

Home

Host

*Concept adapted from LIFE Ministries training materials

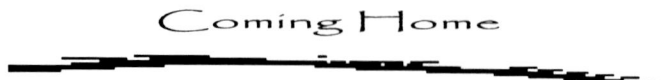

Before we leave home, we fit perfectly in our SQUARE holes because our squareness was developed from the time we were infants, just as their roundness was perfectly developed as they grew, thrived, and adapted to their culture and values. Seldom do we realize that whether we are SQUARES or ROUNDS, when we enter another culture, our values, dreams, desires, and experiences are slightly shaped by the host culture. We quickly learn that in many Asian cultures, we leave our shoes at the door. In some cultures, you don't knock on the door of a house—you cough out in the front yard to announce your presence and so on. After practicing local customs for a period of time, we come back home and are instantly aware of different practices in our home culture. The fact that you remember that different custom proves that you have changed.

We may even discover that we prefer some values or aspects of the host culture. Many returnees enjoy their new values and experiences and love to share them with others. Sometimes they are taken aback when friends and family reject these newly acquired values or practices.

This is proof that now we have now become ROUNDED SQUARES instead of TRUE SQUARES because of our cross cultural experiences. We realize we really don't fit quite as perfectly in our "home culture" holes as we did before. Likewise if one comes from a ROUND culture into our SQUARE culture for some period of time, they may realize upon returning home that they have now become SQUARISH ROUNDS, and they don't exactly fit into their home culture either. It's not about wrong or right—it's about different.

If we don't recognize how we have changed, we can come home with a critical spirit. We can fall into the trap of criticizing or questioning our church's wisdom. If we observed joyful believers in Guatemala who only had two meals per day, it doesn't seem right to purchase carpet for the youth group room or spend thousands to pave the parking lot. If we sat for four hours on a log in an African church service, spending money for padding for the pews seems like a big waste. Remember, before you left for your missions assignment, you would have seen these examples as perfectly appropriate. **It's true—you have changed!**

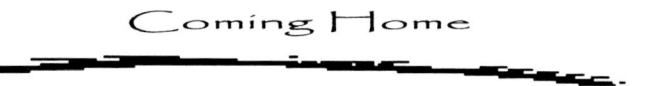

# Take your time

Great drops of sweat soak into the burning sand. We have all seen it on newscasts and films-soldiers carefully, very carefully, probing the soil and inching forward through a minefield or checking for IEDs Progress is painfully slow and deliberate. Sometimes you can see the tension etched on faces, and clothing wet with perspiration. One wrong move and the soldier could become a sudden casualty.

Hours of deliberate, intense, painstaking, and nervewracking work often yield only a few feet of progress. The words of wise instructors ring in the soldier's ears. Training and discipline are essential for success and safety. A soldier who wisely heeds his training and moves carefully and cautiously should succeed.

Getting through reverse culture stress successfully is, in some cases, like inching through a dangerous "no-man's-land." Often we can't see the danger. We can pretend that it's not there, but that doesn't remove it or keep it from impacting us if we fail to take it seriously.

Many factors influence the degree to which reverse culture shock or "reentry stress" impacts each individual. The length of time away from the home culture, the specific situations and culture experienced overseas, individual sensitivities, and a myriad of other influences affect the way each individual reacts. People often find it difficult to believe that they will need to adjust, as they return to the place they call "home."

*For more information see *Reentry Guide for Short-Term Ministry Leaders*, Lisa Espinelli Chinn, Deeper Roots Publications

# What are some of the effects of reentry stress?

## Reentry Stress is often signaled by feelings of:

- *Loneliness*-You feel isolated from family or friends, all alone in a crowd.

- *Being "out of place"*-You don't seem to "fit" anymore.

- *Detachment*-You are watching what is going on, but you're more spectator than participant.

- *Confusion*-Even common situations can create unusual feelings or responses in you.

- *Frustration*-No one understands or even cares how much you want to make a difference, now that you are home.

- *Anger*-Materialism and indifference to things that matter make you angry.

- *Discontentment*-The place you just left seems more like home than the surroundings you have returned to.  You want to "escape."

Which of the above best describes your current feelings?

Before you left your home culture you were happy, comfortable and totally involved in some of the same activities or perspectives that may now frustrate you or "rub you the wrong way."  These unexpected and unsettling feelings may be subtle and may grow more or less intense as time goes on.

Keep trying to realize you are involved in a process.  Identify your feelings, and resist the temptation to feel "special" now that you are back.  Look for your significance in the fact that you are a child of God and not that you served overseas as a missionary.   You must do that by faith.  Our flesh wants to be applauded and uplifted, but God is pleased when we choose the path of humility and servanthood.

*Serve your way to success* and you will begin to understand that God's ways are not our ways. He has wonderful plans for us that are sometimes beyond our wildest dreams.  They usually stay hidden until we begin our quest for truth by acknowledging  and taking action to <u>embrace</u> the reentry process.

# Saying Goodbye

*When Jesus therefore saw his mother, and the disciple standing by, whom he loved, he saith unto his mother, Woman, behold thy son! Then saith he to the disciple, Behold thy mother! And from that hour that disciple took her unto his own home.*
John 19:26-27 KJV

In our culture, saying goodbye is one way we bring closure—a satisfactory conclusion to a time spent with a person or a place. Goodbyes can be both painful and joyful. They can change our lives by ending one phase of our lives and beginning another. This life holds many goodbyes: when we leave family and friends for college, marriage, or the mission field; when we're separated by a major move or extended travel; and when we experience the final earthly separation by the death of a loved one. In the scripture above, Jesus says goodbye to his mother.

Read John 19:25-27. Write down your thoughts concerning a difficult time of saying goodbye. Note relationships and places involved. How did this change your life?

In the NIV translation, the word "dear" is placed before the word "woman." The word "woman" in this verse conveys "great respect." What kind of relationship do you think Jesus had with his mother? In what way did Jesus bring closure to this phase of life for his mother and Himself?

Jesus said goodbye to his dearest friends. In Luke 24:50-53 and Acts 1:9, Jesus knew the importance of bringing closure with final goodbyes and blessing. According to these verses, what did Jesus do to give the disciples a proper closing to the present phase of their lives and a beginning for the next phase?

How do you think the disciples felt as they saw Him leave?

What activities did the disciples enjoy after Jesus departed? What needs were met?

Do you think the disciples would have experienced problems successfully beginning this new phase in their lives if they had not been allowed to see Jesus leave in this manner? Share your thoughts.

Can you think of other things we do in our culture to bring closure? For example, sometimes we give gifts.

Have you terminated any relationships before or during your overseas experience, without a proper and adequate closure? Are these unresolved conflicts that you need to deal with? If you do not carefully pursue satisfactory closure, you may carry burdens, guilt and unrealistic expectations into the next phase of life. Write your plan: perhaps a visit, a card, or a letter. If a death is involved, spend a quiet time sharing your heart with God.

☐ I have accomplished my plan.

## REFLECTING ON YOUR CROSS-CULTURAL EXPERIENCE

How did you feel about leaving your overseas assignment?

Coming Home ©1994, Revised 2007

What were you glad to leave behind?

What was most difficult to leave behind?

## Prayer Suggestion

*Praise the Lord that Jesus is the example for your life. Express to Him any difficulty you are having in bringing an experience or relationship to proper closure. Acknowledge to Him any personal sin that is hindering a relationship. Ask for wisdom to deal with any unresolved conflicts in a godly manner. Praise God for His unconditional love, forgiveness, and acceptance.*

## Insights as you REENTER your home culture
Journaling your thoughts, perspectives, and experiences

# Remember God's Mighty Deeds

DAY 2

*I remembered you, O God, ...I thought about the former days.*  Ps. 77:3, 5a  NIV

At times, God seems so present and so active.  At other times, He seems far away and inactive.  Perhaps you can remember amazing answers to prayer,  or people burdened with seemingly impossible situations experiencing changed hearts or circumstances.  You may have seen others receiving salvation in Christ Jesus.   At this time, however, God's mighty work may not be as evident to you.

Identify three ways in which God clearly showed His direct presence and activity in your life:

1.

2.

3.

The writer of Psalm 77 seemed to view the presence and activity of God as a past experience; this made him feel very troubled.  Read Ps. 77:1-5 and then write in your own words a description of what the Psalmist was going through.

In verse 7-9, the writer expresses his frustration and troubled heart  by asking six questions. How would you answer each of these questions about God?
The writer then begins to think more clearly in verses 10-12.  In verse 10, "the right hand of God" refers to God's might and power.  According to these verses, what has the writer decided to do?

In verses 13-15, what does the Psalmist say about the character and conduct of God? How are these truths about God significant to you?

What is the writer remembering in verses 16-20? How is God's great power expressed?

Do you think the writer is now encouraged? Why? Reread verse 19 and compare this with John 5:17. What does the phrase "though your footprints were not seen" mean to you?

If you are missing the "evident" presence or deeds of God you experienced in the past, how can you, like the Psalmist, encourage yourself in the Lord?

## REFLECTING ON YOUR CROSS-CULTURAL EXPERIENCE

What was the most important thing you learned about God during your time overseas?

Coming Home ©1994, Revised 2007

What do you remember most about the people you served there?

What would you rather forget?

## Prayer Suggestion

*Thank God that, though His "footprints" are not always seen, He is active and is able to work in your life.  Confess any personal sin He has revealed to you.  Praise Him for each truth you listed about Him from verses 13-15.*

## Insights as you REENTER your home culture
### Journaling your thoughts, perspectives, and experiences

Coming Home ©1994, Revised 2007

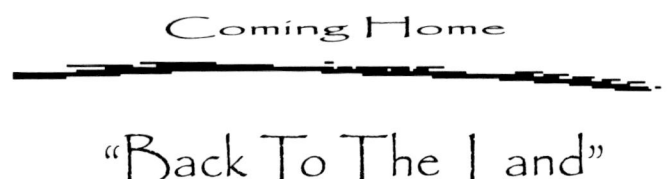

# "Back To The Land"

DAY 3

*With her two daughters-in-law she left the place where she had been living and set out on the road that would take them back to the land of Judah.*  Ruth 1:7  NIV

The book of Ruth begins with Naomi's returning home from a foreign country that was filled with idol worship.  During her absence, many changes took place, both in Moab and in Israel.  This is true for you as you return:  many things have changed; you have changed, and people at home have changed.  Nothing remained the same while you were away.

Read Ruth 1:1-6.  Describe why Elimelich's family left their home country and what took place while they lived there.  What caused Naomi to plan a return to her home in Judah?


In Ruth 1:7-18, deep faith and godliness are revealed in Naomi's life despite a sorrowful and depressed spirit.  As you read, write the phrases that suggest to you Naomi's faith in God even in difficult times.  Did this passage encourage you?  Why?


According to verse 8, what kind of treatment did Naomi and her family receive from her daughters-in-law?


In verse 16,  Ruth says, "Your people will be my people and your God my God."  What does this tell you of Naomi's life and witness while in Moab?


The Moabites were an ungodly group, rejected by God's people.  In spite of that background, what do you observe about Naomi's attitude toward her foreign daughters-in-law?  How will this guide you when you meet people who are different from you or are from another country?

Read Ruth 1:19-21. Naomi's family had left Judah to flee to a foreign country that was despised and rejected by her people. Do you think it was difficult for Naomi to return home? Do you think she expected ridicule and rejection for herself or Ruth, a Moabite? According to verse 19, what was it like when she returned? Were her expectations realized?

How do verses 19-21 express that Naomi had changed? What does Naomi say about this change? (Note: the name Naomi means "sweet and pleasant" and the name Mara means "bitter.")

According to Naomi who was responsible for her great loss and bitter life? (Note: the name "Almighty" emphasizes the great power and provision of God.) Did the loss of Naomi's husband and sons really come from Almighty God? What does the use of God's name "Almighty" show you about how seriously Naomi viewed God?

Even though Naomi felt empty and had experienced much loss, when she returned, she acted responsibly before Almighty God. Because of her obedience, Ruth became God's instrument for healing, blessing, and mercy to Naomi. Read Ruth 4:13-17 to see Ruth's emptiness become fullness, and her bitterness replaced with joy.

Read Matt. 1:1,5-6 and you can observe God's plan for Naomi and Ruth. How does this encourage you?

## REFLECTING ON YOUR CROSS-CULTURAL EXPERIENCE

What encouraged you most from your time overseas?

Is returning home a difficult transition for you? If so, in what way(s)?

What new values are you bringing home with you?

What has been your most frustrating experience or situation since arriving home?

What do you miss most about the people or culture you left behind?

## Prayer Suggestion

*Praise God that "Almighty God" allows the things that come into your life. Confess to God any bitterness you recognize in your life. Thank God for the instant cleansing from sin and restoration of fellowship with Christ. Thank Him for the circumstances, even hard ones, that cause you to depend on His power and provision.*

## Insights as you REENTER your home culture
Journaling your thoughts, perspectives, and experiences

# The Lord Will Sustain You

## DAY 4

*Cast your cares on the LORD and he will sustain you;*
*he will never let the righteous fall.* Ps. 55:22 NIV

When a career or short-term missionary returns home, it is not unusual to be bombarded with old cares and new burdens. Psalm 55:22 is an action-packed verse. The word cast means to throw or hurl your cares or burdens on the Lord with a deliberate mental and spiritual decision. The Lord, as our strength, lovingly desires to step in and carry each burden for us. He responds with action and keeps the believer going; He helps us not to slip or drift off course.

What is your greatest care or burden?

If you continue to carry it alone, could this care or burden cause you to slip and disobey God? What sin or sins could be involved?

Read the following scriptures and write down the ways in which they are an encouragement to you.

1Pet. 5:7

Ps. 37:23-24

Think about the following phrases: He will sustain you..., He will never let the righteous fall ..., He cares for you..., ...for the LORD upholds him with His hand.

Hand in this scripture speaks of Gods power and strength. Consider the person of God who made these statements. Read the following scriptures and write, in your own words, what you learn about God:

Ps. 147:5

2Chr. 16:9a

Matt. 19:26

Rom. 4:21

Which of these scriptures means the most to you? Why?

How can you apply what you have learned about God, through these scriptures, to dealing with the greatest care or burden that you have?

Read Philippians 4:6.

## REFLECTING ON YOUR CROSS-CULTURAL EXPERIENCE

Did you return from your overseas experience with a grateful heart?

List the things for which you are grateful.

While overseas, was there a difficult experience that you now consider with thanksgiving?

## Prayer Suggestion

*Share your deepest concerns with the Lord. Praise Him for His great love, power, and strength that He is willing and able to use on your behalf. Confess to Him any sin that has resulted from carrying the weight of your own cares. Thank Him for the burden, and cast it on Him.*

# Insights as you REENTER your home culture
Journaling your thoughts, perspectives, and experiences

Coming Home ©1994, Revised 2007

# Fret Not

*Fret not thyself because of evildoers, neither be thou envious*
*against the workers of iniquity.* Ps. 37:1  KJV

Evil and the prosperity of those who promote evil often cause the believer to fret.  At times it seems as if God's followers are losing the war.  Many ungodly practices are being promoted as "acceptable" in Christian circles and seem to be prospering.  This can be  extremely discouraging.  Complacency and acceptance of evil has even infiltrated our churches, and it often seems like everything is caving in.  God says, Fret not.

Read Ps. 37:1-2, 9-10   These verses give us insight into the eventual end of the wicked. What is God's instruction to the believer in verse 9?

Read Ps. 37:12-17 to understand God's point of view on this matter of wickedness and the prosperity of the wicked.

God doesn't fret; what does He do?  Why?

The word "arms" in the King James Version denotes strength or power.   What does verse 17 say will happen to the wicked?  What promise is for the believer?

Write the phrases that most encourage you in Ps. 37:12-17.

Ps. 37:1  shows our tendency to envy the wealth and power of the wicked.  What does verse 16 say to you about the riches of the wicked?

Find the solution for fretting in Ps 37:3-8.  Write the first words or phrase of instruction in each verse.

Now turn to John 15:18-27. Jesus teaches His disciples the truth concerning the way of the world and the resulting hardship for the believer. John 16:1 shows how Jesus understands the believer's grief and discomfort in this world and shares why He forewarns them. Read this text and record your thoughts.

In the J. B. Phillips' translation, John 16:1 reads, "I have told you this now so that your faith in me may not be shaken..." The disciples were greatly distressed at their world, and Jesus did not want these deplorable circumstances to shake their faith. Read John 16:6-7. What does Jesus promise these grief-stricken followers?

Jesus was the greatest encourager the world has ever known. He understands our grief about the changes that are taking place in our world. His encouragement to His disciples is found in John 16:20-22. After reading this scripture, write the words of Jesus that most encourage you.

What are the reasons given in these verses for believers to have joy?

## READJUSTING TO YOUR HOME CULTURE

Has anything caused you to "fret" and feel anxious since your return?

What did you see or feel during your cross-cultural experience that caused you to fret or be anxious?

What changes during your absence were noteworthy or difficult for you to adjust to?

Are these experiences in your life turning you toward God with dependence upon His power and provision for you?

## Prayer Suggestion

*Share with God your deepest thoughts concerning any distress you have toward the direction of this world. Express to Jesus how much you appreciate His understanding for how you feel. Thank Him that He is in control of all circumstances, and that they are working toward His planned return. Praise Him for the Holy Spirit-the Comforter-who will guide you into all truth, the truth that will mature and stabilize you in your faith. Thank Him for the joy He promises you.*

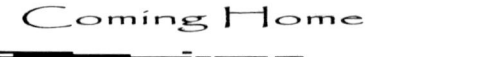
## Insights as you REENTER your home culture
### Journaling your thoughts, perspectives, and experiences

# Speech, Seasoned With Salt

DAY 6

*Let your speech be alway with grace, seasoned with salt,*
*that ye may know how ye ought to answer every man.* Col. 4:6 KJV

This verse could begin, "Let whatever you say always be gracious, kind, and gentle." Kindness and gentleness are truly the examples set by the Lord Jesus in His character and actions.

Salt is a well-known preservative and seasoning. We use preservatives to add to the quality of something and to keep it in good condition. Salt improves the value of that which is seasoned.

Is your conversation always adding to the quality and condition of someone? Does your speech add to the value of, or build up, another?

What changes would come into your life if your communication toward others was always kind and gentle? How is your heart affected when you cut others down?

Read the following verses and write what they mean to you:

Prov. 25:11

Eccl. 10:12

Eph. 4:29

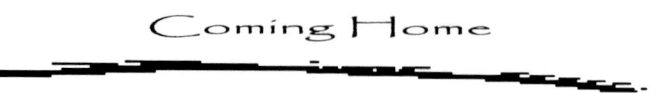

Ps. 19:14

The gracious character of our Lord Jesus Christ is lived through the believer by the Holy Spirit. In Eph. 5:18, we are commanded to be controlled by the Spirit of God. This Spirit control is a reality in the believer's life on a moment-by-moment basis, through obedience. Read Gal. 5:22-26 for the result of this obedience. List the nine traits that affect your speech when you are controlled by the Holy Spirit.

Galatians 5:26 mentions reasons that cause our speech to be ungracious, unkind, and lacking in gentleness. Explain these three areas in your own words. Underline the one that most often causes your conversation to be lacking in graciousness. What steps you will take to correct this?

## READJUSTING TO YOUR HOME CULTURE

Now that you are "home," what experience or change in your own heart attitude has most affected how you speak or what you say to others?

What is the most common response that you receive? Why do you think you get this response?

Evaluate the way you have been communicating your heart attitude and experience with others.

☐ I feel intense, pressured

☐ I give up-no one really cares

☐ I speak kindly and gently, trusting the Lord to communicate through me

☐ Other

## Prayer Suggestion

*If needed, agree with God that you have sinned by failing to be gentle and kind in your conversations with others. Acknowledge your need for moment-by-moment obedience, so that the Holy Spirit is in control in your life. Thank God for His constant willingness to forgive your sins and cleanse you from all unrighteousness.*

# Insights as you REENTER your home culture
Journaling your thoughts, perspectives, and experiences

# "Do You Want To Get Well?"

DAY 7

*When Jesus saw him lying there and learned that he had been in this condition*
*for a long time, he asked him, "Do you want to get well"?* John 5:6  NIV

What a strange question for Jesus to ask.  Read John 5:1-9 to understand the circumstances that brought about such a question.

This man had been sick for 38 years.  Perhaps the man had grown so accustomed to his illness that he was wallowing in self-pity.  Jesus needed him to consider if he really wanted to be free of his illness.  Maybe self-pity was the reason that no one was on hand to carry the man to these healing waters.  When we feel sorry for ourselves, we certainly project an attitude that causes others to avoid us.  Some believe (because of verse 14) that this man's problem was sin, but either way, Jesus seemed to want him to decide if he wanted to escape.

If anyone could have a valid reason to feel sorry for himself and indulge in self-pity,  this man certainly did; but Jesus wanted this man to be well and to glorify God with his life.

Is the sin of self-pity keeping you from glorifying God with your life?  Could you be enjoying and justifying negative feelings and actions in your life that prevent you from obeying God?

Read the following verses and write the words that encourage you.

Ps. 57:1-2

Jer. 29:11-14a  (Read this scripture in context to see what tremendous pressures Israel was under at this time.)

In Jer. 29:11-14a, you can see a reason for the struggles that either tempt us to feel sorry for ourselves and hinder our growth, or else motivate us to trust God and find Him able in every situation. Write the reason(s) and your thoughts.

Sometimes leaving home can be very hard for us, but returning can often be much more difficult. Are you trusting God to be sufficient for every situation that awaits you as you return? The Apostle Paul viewed his circumstances as an opportunity for Christ's power to make itself known through his weaknesses. Read 2 Cor. 12:9-10 and record your thoughts.

Read 1 Ths. 5:18. Does this scripture reveal a key that can help you deal with self-pity? How will you begin to use this key to defeat the sin of self-pity in your life? Memorize this verse.

## READJUSTING TO YOUR HOME CULTURE

Are the following two statements true for you?

1. I am grateful to God for the opportunity to have a short-term or long-term missions experience.

2. I am grateful to God to have returned, and thankful for all that I am experiencing here.

Express why you are, or are not, grateful.

What can you continue to do in a practical sense to deepen your faith and dependence on the Lord?

## Prayer Suggestion

*Consider that you need to act by faith and not allow feelings to control you. Confess your sins of anger, bitterness, self-pity, and/or lack of joy to God. Thank Him that you can be instantly restored into fellowship with Christ according to 1 John 1:9. Thank God for his personal interest and plan for your life. Acknowledge that everything He allows to come into your life is known by Him, and that He works all things for your personal good and benefit.*

## Insights as you REENTER your home culture
Journaling your thoughts, perspectives, and experiences

# Avoiding A Critical Heart

DAY 8

*Do not judge, or you too will be judged.* Matt. 7:1 NIV

Your overseas experience may be the most influential event that has ever taken place in your life. As you return home, you desire to communicate this to others in a meaningful way. Perhaps you even feel a deep spiritual commitment to inform and challenge others to change and get involved. Sometimes, however, you sense only superficial interest from others. There can be a great temptation to find fault and to criticize those who lack understanding. On your return, you may face other people's apathy, indifference, and lack of commitment.

Read Matt. 7:1-5. In these verses, Jesus uses word pictures to help us understand certain principles concerning the correct attitude believers should have when tempted to have a critical heart attitude. Write the meaning of the word picture contained in verses 3-5.

Take time to think carefully. Are you willing to be judged by the same standard by which you judge others?

Perhaps Nathanael displayed a critical, judgmental heart attitude in John 1:43-46. Read this text and see whom he may have misjudged. How did Philip respond to Nathanael's criticism? In what ways can Philip's reply instruct you when you feel negative about someone? Describe practical steps that you could take to have better understanding.

Read Rom. 2:1-2. In your own words, describe what God's Word says is true of those who are critical of others.  How is God's judgment different from how we usually judge others?

Read Rom. 15:5-7 and list phrases that encourage you to have a godly heart attitude.  What are we commanded to do in verse 7?  List the reasons given for this command and the result of obeying it.

Col. 3:13-15 gives us more insight into the proper heart attitude we should have toward others.  In the KJV, the first word is "forbearing."  In the NIV, the word "bear" is used. These words refer to a sense of carrying or supporting one another in the area of spiritual need.  Read this text and list the five commands to believers.

## READJUSTING TO YOUR HOME CULTURE

What did you criticize during your cross-cultural experience?

Now that you are home, of what do you find yourself critical? Why?

What is the difference between a discerning heart and a critical heart?

How do you cultivate the sensitivity to have a discerning heart?

What does Jesus want you to do with your criticism(s) and/or your critical heart?

## Prayer Suggestion

*If you recognize that you have a critical heart attitude toward another person or life situation, agree with God by confessing that attitude as sin. Thank Him that He is never critical of you as a person, but always forgiving. Praise God for His understanding of the special situations and events in your life. Thank Him that He always loves to listen to you. Ask God to work in your life so the five commands in Col. 3:13-15 will continue to mature in your life. Name each one.*

## Insights as you REENTER your home culture
### Journaling your thoughts, perspectives, and experiences

# "Delight Yourself In The Lord"

DAY 9

*Delight yourself in the LORD and he will give you the desires of your heart.*
Ps. 37:4 NIV

"Delight" is defined as "great pleasure." How can we have "great pleasure" in the Lord? Understanding this concept is very important, since He promises that if you delight in Him, "He will give you the desires of your heart." Think for a few minutes and write your ideas of how you can take pleasure in the Lord.

Read the following verses and list the ways the writers took pleasure in the Lord. The words "statutes," "laws," and "words," in these verses refer to the "Word of God."

Neh. 1:11a

(Note: The word "revering" in the NIV as well as the word 'fear' in the KJV means "to show great respect for.")

Ps. 112:1

Ps. 119:24

Ps. 119:35

Ps. 119:143

Isa. 61:10

Jer. 15:16

Ps. 111:2

The Apostle Paul expresses his delight in Rom. 7:22. What was his way of delighting in the Lord? What do you think Paul means by "the inward man" or "my inner being"? Do these phrases indicate an attitude of heart, or an action? Explain your answer.

Examine your previous list carefully. In what ways are you personally delighting in the Lord? Write the practical changes you plan to make in order to take pleasure in your Lord.

The word "desire" in the Hebrew means "to request or ask." What are the desires of your heart? Can you trust God with your desires? Why? Why not? Read the following scriptures and note how they are an encouragement to you.

Ps. 138:8

Isa. 55:9

Jer. 29:11

Jesus shared His heartfelt desire with God the Father in Matt. 26:39,42. Read this familiar passage. Write the phrase that Jesus prayed to ensure that His desires were in obedience to the desires of His Father. What are your thoughts concerning requesting what you desire?

## READJUSTING TO YOUR HOME CULTURE

How will delighting yourself in the Lord "arm you for the battle"?

Do you sense that you are involved in spiritual warfare as you readjust? Why?

## Prayer Suggestion

*Share with your Lord each way He is your delight or how you plan to make Him the delight of your life. Thank God for His commands. Express to Him your joy and delight in obeying His Word. Praise Him that He will give you the desires of "His heart" as He did with His Son.*

## Insights as you REENTER your home culture
### Journaling your thoughts, perspectives, and experiences

# Powerful And Effective Prayer

DAY 10

*The prayer of a righteous man is powerful and effective.*  James 5:16b  NIV

As you return home, you will be faced with many new concerns, values and insights. You must make conscious choices on how you will handle these present challenges. The best option is remembering to pray and trust God with them. In your circumstances, that may be a difficult choice. Many returnees choose detachment. They pull away from their church or others; some choose resentment and bitterness, and break their fellowship with God. These are classic symptoms of reentry stress.

Many believers admit that their greatest spiritual weakness is in the area of prayer. Even with the promise of prayer's "effectiveness," we may remain weak and disobedient to God regarding prayer. Read James 5:17-18. Who does James use as his example of a righteous man that prays? According to this passage, what is true of a righteous man? In what way is this an encouragement to you?

In the KJV, James 5:16b reads, The effectual fervent prayer of a righteous man availeth much. The word "fervent" means "in earnest." Read Acts 12:1-17. Who was praying earnestly and what were they praying for? Which verse shows that though earnest prayer was offered, those who prayed did not really think God would answer their prayers and give them the desire of their hearts?

God answered their prayer because their request was consistent with His will. Did they know that they were praying in His will? How does this example of prayer encourage you to be earnestly praying for your requests?

Righteous Christians are those who have confessed and agreed with God about any personal sin revealed to them by the Holy Spirit. These believers are cleansed from all unrighteousness. Read 1 John 1:9. Describe what each of the following scriptures show about how God acts or feels toward those who are righteous:

Prov. 15:8-9

Prov. 15:26

Prov. 15:29

Ps. 34:15

Ps. 34:17

1Pet. 3:12

Does it encourage you to know that your prayer is powerful, effective, and heard by Almighty God? Take time to think deeply. What concerns will you bring to Him in prayer?

## READJUSTING TO YOUR HOME CULTURE

In what way has your attitude toward prayer changed since returning from overseas?

What changes are occurring now that you are home?

In what way do you think prayer helps you cope with "readjustments" here at home?

## Prayer Suggestion

*Express your thanksgiving to God for hearing the prayers of the righteous. Confess by agreeing with God about any personal sin that the Holy Spirit has revealed to you. Praise Him that your prayers are effective and powerful. Share with confidence the concerns that you listed above. End your prayer with praise for His actions and feelings toward you as one who is righteous.*

## Insights as you REENTER your home culture
### Journaling your thoughts, perspectives, and experiences

Coming Home ©1994, Revised 2007

# God's Heart For All Nations

DAY 11

*... and in thee shall all families of the earth be blessed.* **Gen. 12:3b   KJV**

Nearly every book of the Bible reflects God's desire for all nations to believe in Him.   A "covenant" is an agreement between two parties.   In His covenant with Abraham (i.e., in the Abrahamic Covenant),   God promised that all the "families" or ethnic peoples of the earth would be blessed by the Redeemer.   Read Genesis 12: 2-3.

What part of this covenant has been fulfilled?   The phrase "and in thee shall all families of the earth be blessed" has not yet been fulfilled.

Read Gal. 3:6-9, 14.   In what way is this unconditional covenant a blessing to us?

Have all the nations or peoples heard the gospel so that they may enter into the blessing that God has promised those who come by faith?   What is still needed?

Rom. 10:13-15 reveals to us what is needed to see the blessings of this covenant extend to all the nations and families on the earth.   List four needs from verses 14-15:

1.

2.

3

4.

Name two types of people mentioned in verses 14 and 15 that can be instrumental in the salvation of these lost souls.

Rom. 10:17 tells us how "faith" comes. What must be heard for an unbeliever to become a believer?

Read John 4:35-38. You have the opportunity to "lift up your eyes and look." What do you observe? What does "white already to harvest" mean in verse 37?

In your own words, write of the wonderful truths revealed about reapers and sowers in verses 36-38.

What steps of obedience will you take to see all families of the earth be blessed with the hearing of the gospel of Christ?

## READJUSTING TO YOUR HOME CULTURE

How has your overseas experience affected your desire to be involved in missions either as a GOer or SENDer?

Are any of your life goals changing?

The Bible often speaks of the value of listening to a " multitude of counselors." Who are you looking to for counsel if you are considering new options for your life?

## Prayer Suggestion

*Thank the Lord for His covenant and the opportunity it offers all families of the nations. Express your thanks that those who go, and those who send, are important members of a team to get the gospel to all nations. Praise God for allowing you to have His Word in your language so that you could hear and believe. Praise Him that in the task of sharing the gospel with unbelievers, both those who sow the Word, and those who reap, rejoice together. Share with God your own thoughts concerning this study.*

## Insights as you REENTER your home culture
Journaling your thoughts, perspectives, and experiences

# You Can Make A Difference!

DAY 12

*Don't let anyone look down on you because you are young, but set an example for the believers in speech, in life, in love, in faith and in purity .* 1Tim. 4:12 NIV

The Apostle Paul encourages Timothy to set an example for the believers: in what he says, by his lifestyle, by expressing Christ's love, in a believing faith based on God's Word, and in purity. Like Timothy, you can make a difference now: in your family, in your church, with your friends, and in this needy world.

Paul tells Timothy how to prepare and empower himself to be a good example. Read 1Tim. 4:13. Perhaps you will never be a pastor of a church, as Timothy was, but you can share with others what you are learning and devote yourself to reading and understanding God's Word.

Based on Titus 2:7-8, write ways that you can set a good example.

Has your past example to family, church, and friends been one that exhibited a pattern of good works? Underline the most needy area(s) in your life, and write what you will do to change any inadequate example:

-In what you say:

-In your lifestyle:

-In expressing Christ's love to others:

-In a maturing faith based on God's Word:

-In purity:

Read the following scriptures carefully and write what each says about "good works."

Eph. 2:10

2Tim. 3:16-17

Col. 1:9-10

Phil. 1:6

What has challenged you?

What has encouraged you?

## READJUSTING TO YOUR HOME CULTURE

Can you determine if your cross-cultural experience is helping you form any new perspectives?

Do you think God could use you or your new perspectives to make a difference in your home church and/or family relationships? How?

What would need to change in your life to make you more effective in your family, school, or church situation?

## Prayer Suggestion

*Express to the Lord any fears you may have about being the example to others you need to be. Confess to God the failure in your past example, and ask Him to strengthen and mature you in these areas. Commit yourself to the reading and study of God's Word, so that you may be empowered by His grace to obey as you walk with Him on a moment-by-moment basis. Express your trust in His faithfulness to you.*

# Insights as you REENTER your home culture
Journaling your thoughts, perspectives, and experiences

# God's Will For You!

*For this reason, since the day we heard about you, we have not stopped praying for you and asking God to fill you with the knowledge of his will through all spiritual wisdom and understanding. Col. 1:9 NIV*

Knowing God's will is a priority of every committed believer. We spend valuable hours thinking and praying about major decisions for the future: a college major, a future job or profession, a marriage partner, or where to live. Seeking God's will through prayer is very important. God's will entails far more than decision making for the future. God's will is for NOW!

Read Jer. 9:23-24. Write what you understand to be His will for you. What virtues in verse 23 are useless without the truth of verse 24?

Think of ways that you can get to know someone you haven't met personally.

In Col. 1:9-10, the Apostle Paul prays for believers. What is needed to know God's will? What is the purpose of the "knowledge of His will"?

Your responsibility is to get to know God through His Word and to allow Him to shape and mature you into His image as your relationship with Him develops. As you walk with Him in obedience, on a moment by moment basis, He will make the next steps for your life clear.

Jesus says in John 10:15 ...the Father knows me and I know the Father. Do you know "about" God—or do you "know" Him? What is the difference?

What do the following verses say about how much value Christ put on knowing God?

John 17:3

John 17:25-26

Summarize what you have learned in this lesson. Has your thinking changed about knowing God's will? In what way?

## READJUSTING TO YOUR HOME CULTURE

What steps will you take to further develop your personal relationship with Him?

Often we are "caught by surprise" by the changes in our attitude and circumstances. Check below if you are currently experiencing "feelings" like:

- ☐ Nobody seems to care
- ☐ Irritation / anger
- ☐ Being "out of phase" with current values
- ☐ Disillusionment
- ☐ Bewilderment
- ☐ Too many choices / decisions hard to make
- ☐ Materialism reigns
- ☐ Frustration
- ☐ People are not interested
- ☐ Other

Realize that you are reentering a culture where the emphasis is on getting things done "on time." How do you express the value of people over productivity?

Have you formed any new perspectives about God's will for your life?

## Prayer Suggestion

*Share with God your desire to mature and develop in your relationship with Him. Express to Him the steps you plan to take to know Him better. Confess every known personal sin that has kept you from growing spiritually. Praise the Lord that the Holy Spirit gives knowledge, spiritual wisdom, and understanding as you study God's Word. Thank the Lord that He cares for you and wants to lead you step by step into a better understanding of His will.*

# Insights as you REENTER your home culture
## Journaling your thoughts, perspectives, and experiences

# 100% Guaranteed Success

DAY 14

*Do not let this Book of the Law depart from your mouth; meditate on it day and night,
so that you may be careful to do everything written in it. Then you
will be prosperous and successful.* Josh. 1:8 NIV

Written across the classroom blackboard were the words, "If I could give you a 100% guaranteed method for success in your life—would you do it?" These words followed several days of teaching on the many kings of the Bible who began well but ended their lives in disobedience and defeat before God. True spiritual success is greatly desired by committed believers and is absolutely obtainable.

Read about God's promise to Joshua in Joshua 1:5-9. Think carefully about verse 9. The word "meditate" means "deep and serious thought." Write in your own words God's method for spiritual success.

What does God promise in verses 5 and 9 that will assure you of spiritual success? Hebrews 13:5b contains the same promise. What does this truth mean to you?

Read and meditate on the following verses, and record your thoughts about each. Remember that when the "law" is mentioned in these verses, you can substitute "the Word of God."

Ps. 1:2-3

Ps. 119:72

Ps. 119:97

Ps. 119:148

John 16:13   But when he, the Spirit of truth, comes, he will guide you into all truth. How does this verse encourage you to spend time thinking deeply and seriously about scripture?

Do you take time to think deeply and seriously on the scriptures and verses found in the Word of God?  What steps will you take to improve and assure your spiritual success?

## READJUSTING TO YOUR HOME CULTURE

How are you trusting God to meet your emotional and spiritual needs as you readjust?

List three things that you are willing to surrender to the Lord as you readjust:

1.


2.


3.



Note three ways that you can express your gratefulness to the Lord during your readjustment period:

1.


2.


3.



## Prayer Suggestion

*Express to God your desire for true spiritual success. Confess, by naming specifically, any personal sin that blocks your path to success. Praise and thank the Lord for His powerful Word that is available in your language. Pray for the many peoples who are yet without the Word of God in their language. Thank Him for the Holy Spirit, who will guide you into all truth. Praise Him that He will never leave you or desert you.*

# Coming Home

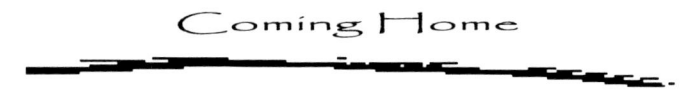

# YOUR FINAL CHALLENGE

## READJUSTING TO YOUR HOME CULTURE

Amid incredible schedules, commitments and obligations, you are now faced with your most important challenge since coming home from your overseas experience!

1.  Find a quiet place and spend a minimum of 1 to 2 hours (more if possible) of <u>undisturbed</u> time reflecting on your overseas experiences. Leave familiar surroundings if you need to.

2.  On the following pages write as much as you can about the Lord, lessons you've learned, and ways you have changed?

3.  Document your desire and an action plan to preserve your new and different outlook, and perspectives on life.

4.  Sign and date your journal page when you have completed this assignment.

5.  Share you current thoughts and feelings with someone you trust (preferably someone with overseas experience who understands the reentry transition that you are going through).

## Insights as you REENTER your home culture
### Journaling your thoughts, perspectives, and experiences

_____

_____

_____

_____

_____

_____

_____

_____

_____

_____

_____

_____

_____

_____

_____

_____

_____

_____

# Insights as you REENTER your home culture
Journaling your thoughts, perspectives, and experiences

# Insights as you REENTER your home culture
Journaling your thoughts, perspectives, and experiences

**BEFORE YOU GO**–Preparaton For Short-Term Mission, (Revised 2009)

*Howard Erickson,* Deeper Roots Publications

This newly revised resource is written primarily for those who will be organizing or leading a trip. The 120 page manual has practical tips on making travel arrangements, communicating with host missionaries and packing. It also includes a helpful section on using media to communicate the value of the trip to friends and supporters. Based on years of travel with short-term missions teams, *Before You Go* is designed to save time and effort for beginners and pros alike
BYG...$10.95

## Devotional Bible Studies

### PRE-FIELD PREPARATION,
Spiritual Focus Before You Go

*Howard & Bonnie Lisech,*
Deeper Roots Publications

These (Book 1 & Book 2) devotional Bible studies are specifically designed for the Pre-Field training of STM individuals and teams. Each devotional is written to help team members grow spiritually and evaluate their attitudes and actions *before* they leave on a Short-Term Missions trip. Just as a pilot has to PRE-FLIGHT his plane before committing his life and the lives of his passengers to the take-off, we need to make sure that we deliberately prepare and *"pre-flight"* our hearts for service in another culture. Spiritual preparation is ESSENTIAL to gain the most from the STM experience. *7 day (stapled) or 14 day (spiral bound) editions are available.*
668PFP-14....$6.95, 669PFP-7....$4.50, 671PFP2-7....$4.50

### WALK AS HE WALKED
– On-Field Book 1 of 4 different Devotional Bible Studies for various trip lengths.

*Howard & Bonnie Lisech,*
Deeper Roots Publications

*Walk as He Walked*, first in a series of 4 different devotional Bible studies/spiritual journals, earned an endorsement by Elisabeth Elliot!
Designed for both full time and short-term missionaries, they will add an important dimension to any cross-cultural experience. Thousands have used them with great success. Topics are sequenced for the culture shock curve and

missionary usage, but many other believers are using them for personal refreshment and time with God.
*14 day, 21 day, 30 day, and 50 day editions are available.*
601WAHW-50......$11.95      602 WAHW-30........$9.95
603WAHW-21......$8.95       604WAHW-14......$6.95

### ABIDE IN THE VINE,
*Howard & Bonnie Lisech,*
Deeper Roots Publications

These spiritual journals and devotional Bible studies are endorsed by Don Richardson and are great for those who finish *Walk as He Walked*. These too, were designed for short-term missionaries and will add an important dimension to any STM trip experience. Topics are sequenced for the culture shock curve and missionary usage, but some laymen and church leaders are using them for personal refreshment and time with God. *50 day, 21 day, and 14 day editions are available.*
621AITV-50....$11.95    623AITV21....$8.95   624AITV14....$6.95

### RIPE FOR HARVEST,
*Howard & Bonnie Lisech,*
Deeper Roots Publications

***Ripe for Harvest*** is great for those who have finished ***Walk as He Walked,*** or ***Abide in the Vine,*** while on a missions trip. These devotional Bible study/spiritual journals will add an important dimension to any STM experience. Topics are sequenced for the culture shock curve and missionary usage. They were written for those who have completed multiple STM trips but, like the others, many people are using them for personal devotions. *14 day, and 21 day editions are available.*
643RFH-21....$8.95          644RFH-14....$6.95

### LIVE IN THE LIGHT – On-Field Book 4 of 4
*Howard & Bonnie Lisech,* Deeper Roots Publications

***Live In The Light*** is brand NEW devotional Bible study/spir! Fourth in the *On-Field* series it is written for those who travel on multiple STM trips and have completed ***Walk as He Walked, Abide in the Vine,*** or ***Ripe for Harvest.*** This helpful resource will add an important dimension to any STM experience.
As in the first 3 books, topics are sequenced for the culture shock curve and will be welcomed by both long and short-term missionaries. Journal pages are provided. Others will use them for personal devotions as well. *14 day edition is available.*
#640LITL-14....$6.95

## Four Essential Reentry Resources

### COMING HOME – REENTRY BOOK 1

*Howard & Bonnie Lisech,* Deeper Roots Publications

Thousands of short-term and long-term missionaries have completed **Coming Home** or *Fishers of Men* reentry devotionals with excellent results. The devotional studies and *focused reentry questions* help anyone returning home as they begin readjusting to their own culture. **Coming Home** is especially helpful for those who have completed the **Walk as He Walked, Abide in the Vine,** or **Ripe for Harvest** on-field devotional studies. Several mission agencies provide this book for their missionaries returning from life in a different culture.                651CH...$6.95

### COMING HOME AGAIN– REENTRY BOOK 2

*Howard & Bonnie Lisech,* Deeper Roots Pubs.

**Coming Home Again** Book 2 is another 14 day reentry devotional Bible study. It is appropriate for those who have *ALREADY* used the *Coming Home* (*Fishers of Men*) reentry devotionals during their first reentry experience. As people return to their home culture from overseas assignments for the second time, this book provides necessary help. Reentry stress is a real issue and returnees need effective tools to help minimize its effects. Lisa Espinelli Chinn says, "*Coming Home Again* is another great resource for help with readjustment to our home culture after a second or third short-term or long-term mission experience."      652CHA-14..$6.95

### RETURNING HOME– REENTRY BOOK 3   NEW!

*Howard & Bonnie Lisech,* Deeper Roots Publications

**Returning Home** is a brand new 14 day *Reentry* devotional! It was written especially for those who have *ALREADY* used **Coming Home** or **Coming Home Again**. Some people return to their home culture without realizing that they have changed during their cross-cultural experience. The devotionals and focused reentry questions in this new volume will help smooth the transition back to the home culture. #658RH-14....$6.95

### REENTRY GUIDE FOR SHORT-TERM MISSION LEADERS, Lisa Espinelli Chinn,
Deeper Roots Publications

Lisa Espinelli Chinn is an authority on *Reentry Stress*. In this book she provides valuable insights and instructions on how to successfully deal with it after your trip. This important publication contains her research, ideas, and concepts that can help you assist your team members return successfully. Nine important chapters, plus four exercises in the appendix, make this small but powerful 76 page book an essential tool in your chest of resources to help you and your team have a succesful reentry.

#653RGSTML.......$10.95

## 3 books combined into ONE volume

### LIVE IN THE LIGHT COMBO BOOK

*Howard & Bonnie Lisech,* Deeper Roots Pubs   NEW!

At last! *ONE volume containing 7 prefield, 14 On-Field, and 14 Reentry devotional Bible study/ spiritual journals.* Totally new material written with todays' STMers in mind. This innovative volume will help your team members grow spiritually during all 3 phases of the STM missions experience. Help guide those you are sending to a closer walk with God by engaging them with enriching devotional Bible studies presented in an appealing yet inexpensive format. Maximize their STM experience by providing 35 days of *quality* spiritual input for less than 1% of the average overseas per-person trip cost.

#641LITLcombo.... $13.50

## 2 books combined into ONE volume

Choose from the 14 or 21 day editions of **Walk as He Walked, Abide in the Vine** or **Ripe for Harvest (On-Field devotionals)** to be bound together with the 14 day **Coming Home (Reentry devotional)** into a single convenient ministry tool.

*Enhance the spiritual impact of both the overseas portion and the reentry portion of your short term experience with a single inexpensive resource.* These compact books take the previously described materials for overseas trips and bind them together with the **Coming Home** or **Coming Home Again** reentry materials to make COMBINATION books. These books help with both on-field *culture shock* and dealing with *reentry stress* as team members return home and face the inevitable adjustments.

### WALK AS HE WALKED/COMING HOME COMBO
#613wahw14/CH..$11.50   #612wahw21/CH..$13.50

### ABIDE IN THE VINE/COMING HOME & COMING HOME AGAIN COMBO
#627aitv14/CH...$11.50   #626aitv21/CH....$13.50
#628aitv14/CHA....$11.50

### RIPE FOR HARVEST/COMING HOME & COMING HOME AGAIN COMBO
647RFH14/ch....$11.50   646rfh21/ch....$13.50
648RFH14/cha..$11.50

NEW!

### HELPING HANDS–HEALING HEARTS– BOOK 1 AND BOOK 2
*Howard & Bonnie Lisech,* Deeper Roots Publications

These two different devotional Bible study/journals are especially written with *medical health teams* in mind. They were originally developed for an organization that sends over a thousand medical personnel overseas annually. The devotionals are shortened to fit the restrictive time frames so common on the field. Each book includes 8 *Pre-Field,* 14 *On-Field,* and 8 *Reentry* devotionals covering all 3 essential phases of each trip bound in a single volume with scripture text included.

633HelpHand1...$11.50
634HelpHand2...$11.50

# SAWYER®

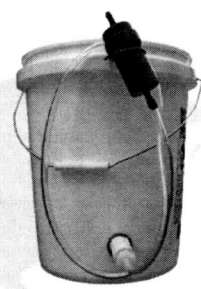

## The **fastest**, **easiest** and most **cost efficient** way to get potable **WATER**

Using technology taken from kidney dialysis, Sawyer® Water Filters use Hollow Fiber Membranes. Our filters are comprised of tiny "U" shaped hoses that allow the water to enter into their core through tiny micro pores. The 0.1 micron absolute pores in the biological filter are so small that no bacteria, protozoa, or cysts like E.Coli, Cholera and Typhoid can get through. In fact, at 7 log (99.99999%) this is the highest level of filtration available today and yet it has a very high flow rate due to the large amount of hoses. If viruses are an issue we have a 0.02 micron purifier that is the first and thus far only portable filtration device to physically remove viruses, which it does at a >5.5 log (99.9997%) rate exceeding EPA and NSF recommendations. Each filter is certified for ABSOLUTE microns. That means there will be no pore size larger than 0.1 microns in the biological filter and 0.02 microns in the viral purifier.

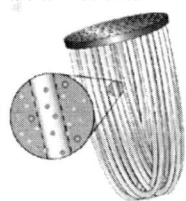

## These are **PERPETUAL** filters. **YOU NEVER HAVE TO REPLACE THE FILTER MEMBRANE**

**Highest Filtration Rates Available-** At 0.1 micron absolute, it is **impossible** for any bacteria, protozoa or cysts to pass through the filter and at 0.02 micron absolute, it is **impossible** for viruses in addition to bacteria, protozoa and cysts to pass through the purifier. These are true barrier filters.

**Simple Design and Construction-** We've made it as simple as it gets. Families would be able to construct and adapt their filter in literally minutes to locally found containers. The kit includes everything you need to attach the filter to any bucket or plastic container. (Bucket not included)

1. *Find a clean bucket or plastic container*
2. *Drill the hole 1.5 inches from the bottom of the bucket (you can do this by hand)*
3. *Screw the adapter and hosing on*
4. *Fill the bucket and let gravity do the rest*

*NEWEST TECHNOLOGY!*

### Kit Contents:

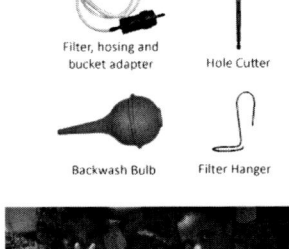

Filter, hosing and bucket adapter

Hole Cutter

Backwash Bulb

Filter Hanger

**Extremely cost efficient-**One system could provide clean water for a small village for pennies a day.

**Fast Flow-** This is a POINT OF USE SYSTEM. Since there is such a high flow rate, this eliminates the need to store water which reduces the chances of water being contaminated after it is filtered. The only external energy source required for the system to function is GRAVITY. The 0.1 micron filter has a flow rate of about 1 liter per minute while the 0.02 micron purifier flows at a rate of approximately .5 liter per minute.

**Easy Maintenance-** Maintenance of this filter is very simple. When the filter starts to slow down or clog, simply back wash it with clean water using the cleaning bulb provided in the kit. YOU NEVER HAVE TO REPLACE THE FILTER MEMBRANE. The ease of operating this system makes it self-sustainable and dependable.

**Natural Disasters-** The bucket system is essential for aid in natural disasters. This system would eliminate the need to ship bottled water.

POINT**ONE** FILTER ( Available from Deeper Roots - **www.DeeperRoots.com** ) POINT**TWO**™

Brochure & Indep. lab test results available upon request. • E-mail: DeeperRoots@aol.com • 407.797.8557 cell

( Available from Deeper Roots - **www.DeeperRoots.com** )

# SAWYER®

# BUCKET FILTER SYSTEMS

Excellent for any Homeland Emergency Preparedness situation (natural or man-made).
Great for STM Teams traveling overseas. (Leaving this behind after the team leaves can provide the *wonderful gift* of SAFE WATER for an entire village or community!)

Complete Water Kits - Attaches to any standard 5 gallon plastic bucket or comparable water container

Simple - Assembles in less than 2 minutes

Durable - **Million gallon guarantee!**

Hollow Fiber Filter - Technology developed from medical Kidney Dialysis

NEWEST TECHNOLOGY!

|  | Viral Purifier | Biological Filter |
| --- | --- | --- |
| Time to filter 5 gallons of water | 42 minutes, | 13.33 minutes |
| Gallons per day | 170 gallons | 540 gallons |
| Gallons per year | 62,000 gallons | 197,000 gallons |
| Gallons in 5 years | 310,000 gallons | 985,000 gallons |
| Cost per day | 4 cents | 2 cents |
| Cost per Gallon | 0.02 cents | 0.004 cents |
| Gallons per penny | 40 gallons | 250 gallons |

**Viral Purification:** The first and thus far only portable filtration device to physically remove viruses. Which it does at a >5.5 log (99.9997%) rate exceeding EPA recommendations.This purifier also removes 7 log (99.99999%) of all bacteria like salmonella, cholera, and E. coli. And 6 log (99.9999%) of all Protozoa such as Giardia and Cryptosporidium.

Biological Filtration: removes 7 log (99.99999%) of all bacteria like salmonella, cholera, and E. coli. And 6 log (99.9999%) of all Protozoa such as Giardia and Cryptosporidium.

$5.00 off any filter or purifier

Deeper Roots website Promo Code: **WF500**

This filter does not remove salt, pesticides, or minerals

Viral & Biological Purifier MSRP $139.99

DRP price $142.00

Biological Filter MSRP $55.99

DRP price $57.00

# www.DeeperRoots.com (in the Missions Resources folder)

Independent lab test results available upon request. • E-mail: DeeperRoots@aol.com • Questions - Howard Lisech 407.797.8557 cell

# 10th, 11th, or 12th Grade Bible Curriculum

### ROOTED & GROUNDED, A Guide for Spiritual Growth
Suitable for 10th or 11th or12th Grade
*Howard & Bonnie Lisech and Jan Harris,* Deeper Roots Publications

This Bible curriculum is being used for a *full year* of Home School or Christian high school Bible classes. It can also be used for college, adult, discipleship, or small group Bible studies. Featuring 27 of Julie Bosacker's beautiful sketches, an unreached people group begins each week's Bible study. Students are introduced to world missions as they move from biblical knowledge to spiritual application in these topical studies. Encouragement for Christian living is presented in an appealing and easy-to-use format. The Teacher's Guide makes teaching easier since all the preparation is completed for you as the teacher. The Student Workbook has room to write the answers and fill in the blanks.

101RGTG Teacher's Guide...$39.50, 102RGSW Student's Workbook...$23.95, 103RGTEST Unit Tests & Answer Keys ...$3.95

# 7th, 8th, or 9th Grade Bible Curriculum

### DISCOVERING OUR AMAZING GOD,
7th, 8th, or 9th Grade Bible Curriculum
(Book 1)
*Jan L. Harris, Howard & Bonnie Lisech,*
This exciting 7th or 8th or 9th Grade Bible curriculum deliberately focuses on some of the less familiar stories and events in the Bible to give students a new appreciation of how much God loves them. Interesting line drawings and suggested activities intermingled with inductive Bible study will help keep students focused. At the beginning of each lesson we introduce beautiful artwork and an unreached people group profile to broaden each student's understanding of our world. The Tch Guide provides extensive notes and will help teachers teach essential biblical truths effectively with a minimum of preparation! The Student Workbook includes reflections/journal pages to help students organize and record their new appreciation for our amazing God.

201DGHSTG Home School (Teacher's Guide)...$28.95

202DGHSSW Home School (Student Workbook) ...$19.95

204DGCSTG Christian School (Teacher's Guide)...$28.95

205DGCSSW Christian School (Student Workbook).....$19.95

### DISCOVERING CHRIST–LIKE HABITS,
7th, 8th, or 9th Grade Bible Curriculum
(Book 3)
*Jan L. Harris, Howard & Bonnie Lisech,*
*Discovering Christ–like Habits* is the third book in our DISCOVERING... series and it is designed to change your student's life patterns. It provides not only a deeper understanding of Christian habits, but also daily practice in such disciplines as prayer, worship, Bible study, etc. The lessons combine Bible studies with plenty of hands-on activities, writing stories, interviewing family members, planning and acting out Bible dramas, and taking a field trip, for example. Your students will gain practical, godly habits while deepening their relationship with Jesus. At the beginning of each lesson, we introduce beautiful artwork and an unreached people group profile to broaden each student's understanding of our world.

221DHHSTG Home School (Teacher's Guide)...$28.95

222DHHSSW Home School (Student Workbook) ...$19.95

224DHCSTG Christian School (Teacher's Guide)...$28.95

225DHCSSW Christian School (Student Workbook).....$19.95

### DISCOVERING WHO I AM IN CHRIST,
7th, 8th, or 9th Grade Bible Curriculum
(Book 2)
*Jan L. Harris, Howard & Bonnie Lisech,*
Second in the "Deeper Roots Discovering..." series, book 2 of this exciting curriculum will help Jr. High students understand their identity in Christ. This life changing principle is the focus of this exciting new curriculum. It, too, has drawings, cartoons, and suggested activities intermingled with inductive Bible study to challenge and help students. The Teacher's Guide and Student Workbook are similar in layout and function to those found in Book 1. Each lesson also introduces an unreached people group to interest and help your students.

211DCHSTG Home School (Teacher's Guide)...$28.95

212DCHSSW Home School (Student Workbook) ...$19.95

214DCCSTG Christian School (Teacher's Guide)...$28.95

215DCCSSW Christian School (Student Workbook)...$19.95

### DISCOVERING A CHRIST–LIKE CHARACTER,
7th, 8th, or 9th Grade Bible Curriculum
(Book 4)
*Jan L. Harris, Howard & Bonnie Lisech,*
*Discovering A Christ–like Character* is the final book in the DISCOVERING... series. It uses Bible accounts of Christ's life to challenge your students to a lifetime of following His example. As they focus on the character of Jesus, such as His compassion, mercy, forgiveness, and patience, they will be drawn to Him and desire to be more like Him. The first chapter covers "Discovering Christlike Joy" and the final chapter is "Christlike Love." Other chapters include lessons on integrity, self-control, humility, and forgiveness. *(May also be used for some 10th graders)*

231DHHSTG Home School (Teacher's Guide)...$28.95

232DHHSSW Home School (Student Workbook) ...$19.95

234DHCSTG Christian School (Teacher's Guide)...$28.95

235DHCSSW Christian School (Student Workbook).....$19.95

## FIRM FOUNDATIONS: CREATION TO CHRIST

CHILDREN'S EDITION, *McLlwain/Everson* (NTM)

Teacher's Manuals

Chronological Bible study from Creation to Christ for Children.

A full year of lessons! This 5- book set of teacher's manuals is ideal for Christian schools, home schooling and children's Bible teachers. Designed for reading aged children, this set parallels the 50 lessons in the adult course of Firm Foundations: Creation to Christ. Each lesson has a review and a skit that can be photocopied. Wonderful teacher helps, including valuable Maps, excellent Timeline Chart, and sequenced Posters, are included with this 5-book set.

301FF5TM....$54.95

## CREATION TO CHRIST

Children's Workbook

Workbook for Creation to Christ Children's Bible Study.

This workbook is designed with 4th and 5th graders in mind but it can be used with up to 6th graders. Each lesson includes a skit and a worksheet for the kids. It is helpful in both the classroom setting and the home school setting. Each workbook contains all 50 lessons.

302FFCSW....$5.95

## BLACK & WHITE LINE DRAWINGS

Set of (112) NTM

Created from the same art work as the color pictures for the Firm Foundations: Creation to Christ Bible curriculum, this 112 picture set (reproducible) is ideal for coloring. Permission is given to copy these pictures for classroom use. These pictures are also available on the NTM Firm Foundations CD. 6"x 8" B&W line drawings

308(6x8)LD........$14.95

## COLOR CHRONOLOGICAL BIBLE TEACHING PICTURES

NTM

These 105 carefully researched and Biblically accurate LAMINATED color pictures will add interest and eye contact to your lessons and will help the Bible stories to come alive. 8.5" x 11" Laminated

304(8.5x11)L....$38.95

## FIRM FOUNDATIONS BIBLE PICTURE CD

105 Chronological Pictures NTM

This valuable CDROM has the 105 color chronological pictures *PLUS* 112 B&W line drawings in BMP, JPG, and CGM format. Comes with Kudo Reader which is easy to install and use for convenient viewing. Includes 105 chronological Bible story color and B&W pictures/line drawings. Print out the Bible story pictures to help illustrate what you are teaching in the Firm Foundations curriculum and for younger children to color. PC/MAC compatible.

307CDBiblePic....$19.95

## ENCOURAGEMENT FOR HOME SCHOOL MOMS

*Bonnie Lisech,* Deeper Roots Publications

Devotional Bible studies that give encouragement and hope. These spiral bound studies, written by a mom who home schooled her children, address the issues and pressures experienced by those who have chosen to educate their children at home. *Encouragement For Home School Moms* was written to help busy moms avoid putting off and missing their special time with God.

105EHSM.....$7.75

## FRUIT THAT REMAINS — Spiritual Growth Through Life Experience,
*Bonnie Lisech,* Deeper Roots Publications

Bonnie challenges readers to view life's blessings, trials, and tests as important steps in spiritual growth. Enjoy the discovery of spiritual principles that lead us to bear Fruit That Remains through an intimate relationship and fellowship with God.

Bonnie Lisech has been studying Scripture, writing, and teaching spiritual truth for over 20 years. She delights in encouraging people around the world. Bonnie writes for Deeper Roots Publications, PIONEERS, and Women of the Harvest Ministries International.

Bonnie says, *"My goals are to challenge women to grow in their faith and to see them enjoy God's sovereignty, love, and power in all circumstances of life."*

107Fruit........$11.95

# ORDERS

**Deeper Roots Publications**
2100 Red Gate Rd.
Orlando, FL 32818

**WWW.DEEPERROOTS.COM**

Phone:(407) 797-8557or
E-mail your order to:
DeeperRoots@aol.com

**Ordered By:**

Name _____

Street address_____

City_____

State/Ctry_____ ZIP _____

Daytime phone ( ) _____

**Ship To:** (only if different from ordered by)

Name _____

Street address_____

City_____

State/Ctry_____ ZIP _____

Daytime phone ( ) _____

## Your personal check, money order, or credit card payment is acceptable.

☐ Visa  ☐ Master Card  ☐☐☐☐ ☐☐☐☐ ☐☐☐☐ ☐☐☐☐

Expiration ☐☐☐☐   3 Digit code (back of card) ☐☐☐

## ORDER ONLINE AT WWW.DEEPERROOTS.COM

| Qty | Stock # | Item | Price Each | Total Price |
|---|---|---|---|---|
| | | | | |
| | | | | |
| | | | | |

All prices are in U.S. funds and are subject to change without notice

USA Postage and Handling Rates:
Call for 2nd and next day rates

| | Media Mail | Priority Mail | UPS Ground |
|---|---|---|---|
| Up to $12.00 | $2.40 | $4.75 | $6.00 |
| $12.01-$30.00 | $5.10 | $6.95 | $7.95 |
| $30.01-$50 | $6.75 | $8.95 | $9.95 |
| $50.01-$100 | 10% | 13% | 18% |
| $100 and up | 8% | 15% | 16% |
| | Post Office 1-3 weeks | Requires 2 to 3 business days | 4-7 business days (not available in AK, HI, or PR) |

| | |
|---|---|
| Florida deliveries add 6.5% Sales Tax | |
| Postage and Handling (see chart at left) | |
| Media Mail (1-3 weeks ) | |
| UPS Ground (4-7 business days ) Not available in AK, HI, or PR | |
| Priority Mail (3-4 business days) | |
| **TOTAL** | |

OVERSEAS Shipping: Email us for shipping costs.

## If you e-mail your order, please include quantity, stock #, your e-mail, and your telephone number.